REPTILES AND AMPHIBIANS OF PRINCE EDWARD COUNTY, ONTARIO

REPTILES AND AMPHIBIANS OF PRINCE EDWARD COUNTY, ONTARIO

Peter Christie

✳ **Natural Heritage Books**

Reptiles and Amphibians
of Prince Edward County, Ontario
© 1997 Peter Christie, Picton, Ontario

Published by Natural Heritage/Natural History Inc.
P.O. Box 95, Station O, Toronto, Ontario M4A 2M8
First Edition

Canadian Cataloguing in Publication
Christie, Peter
    Reptiles and amphibians of Prince Edward County
Includes bibliographical references and index.
ISBN 1-896219-27-6

1. Reptiles - Ontario - Prince Edward - Identification
2. Amphibians - Ontario - Prince Edward - Identification
I. Title.
QL644.C47 1997   597.9'0873'587   C97-931102-0

Graphic Production by Steve Eby
Printed and bound in Canada by Hignell Printing Limited, Winnipeg, Manitoba

Natural Heritage/Natural History Inc. acknowledge the support of the Canada Council for the Arts for our publishing program. We also acknowledge with gratitude the assistance of the Association for the Export of Canadian Books, Ottawa, and the Office of the Ontario Arts Council, Toronto as well as the following supporting groups and organizations.

EHJV·PCHE
EASTERN HABITAT JOINT VENTURE
LE PLAN CONJOINT DES HABITATS DE L'EST
ONTARIO

THE CANADA COUNCIL FOR THE ARTS SINCE 1957 | LE CONSEIL DES ARTS DU CANADA DEPUIS 1957

Canards Illimités Canada
Ducks Unlimited Canada

To my father,
who, by turning stones and woodland logs,
uncovered his gift of curiosity
that all of us carry still.

CONTENTS

ACKNOWLEDGEMENTS

This book was made possible thanks in part to the generous financial assistance of Ducks Unlimited, the Ontario Ministry of Natural Resources and Environment Canada.

The volume also owes a considerable debt to Priscilla Ferrazzi for her wade through the data and her valuable work on the text.

Similarly, Michael J. Oldham, herpetologist with the Natural Heritage Information Centre of the Ontario Ministry of Natural Resources, deserves special mention here. Mr. Oldham initiated the extraordinary task of compiling records for Ontario reptiles and amphibians in 1984 and has continued the work to the present, despite varying interest and elusive funding. He generously provided this project with his Ontario Herpetofaunal Summary data so far accumulated for Prince Edward County. He also provided valuable comments on the manuscript.

I am also grateful to Francis R. Cook, former curator of herpetology at the National Museum of Natural Science (now the Canadian Museum of Nature), for his review of the text and for arranging for me to peruse the museum's records.

Thanks to Thomas A. Huff, former director of the Reptile Breeding Foundation in Cherry Valley, Todd Norris, district ecologist with the Ontario Ministry of Natural Resources in Kingston, Amy Chabot of the Long Point Bird Observatory and anyone else who had a hand in helping me draw together the information that appears here. My indebtedness extends to all those who contributed and continue to contribute to the Ontario Herpetofaunal Summary and to Penny Briggs and the others who participated with me in the Prince Edward County Reptile and Amphibian Survey of 1979. My thanks also goes to Bonaventure (Frank) Saptel and Melanie Willis.

A final note of gratitude I extend to my father, the late W.J. (Jack) Christie, who, as a fisheries biologist and ecological consultant, never let reptiles and amphibians slip from the periphery of his ecological vision. His short list of things I could do around the house sparked this project.

INTRODUCTION

Prince Edward County has an impressive diversity of reptiles and amphibians for its northern latitude. It boasts records (confirmed and possible) for some 30 of Ontario's 50 species. The inclusive range of other reptiles and amphibians suggest this complement may be even larger.

Unfortunately, this fact is not well known; reptiles and amphibians are often vilified or absent from the amateur naturalist's repertoire of interest. Concern for them is frequently displaced by concern for birds and other larger, more aesthetically palatable animals.

But reptiles and amphibians occupy a special place among Prince Edward County fauna, particularly as they reflect the area's unique ecology and its delicate wetlands. Further, their changing populations can be useful for evaluating the impact of shifts in land use throughout the area. Developments within populations of amphibians, especially, are increasingly being recognized in many places as important indices of ecological health.

This volume is written in the hope of increasing awareness of locally found reptiles and amphibians. Its broadest purpose is to contribute to an understanding of their place as little-known residents of the County. It is also to impart some appreciation of the impressive wealth of wetlands in the area so that we can work to conserve them.

The descriptions and illustrations provided in this book are meant as an elementary guide to identification. Several quality field guides are widely available for better identifying the reptiles and amphibians found in the County and the regions around it. Similarly, detailed information about the natural history of each animal is not included here and is best found elsewhere (see references on page 116).

The principal intent of this book, rather, is to provide an accumulated account of the reptile and amphibian records compiled for Prince Edward County from past and present observations and collections. It is a book about the presence, absence and abundance of these intriguing animals. As a guide, it is mainly to illustrate the distribution of reptiles and amphibians so far encountered in this area.

Prince Edward County reptiles and amphibians have the distinction of having been perhaps more carefully scrutinized than those of many other areas. For instance, more than half-a-century ago, researchers from the Royal Ontario Museum spent a summer collecting information about County wildlife for a faunal survey of the area. E.B.S. Logier wrote the survey's account of County reptiles and amphibians.

Some three-and-a-half decades after that study was published, a team of students tramped through the area's marshes and woodlands, measuring, weighing and describing the County's reptiles and amphibians for an entire summer in 1979. That study provided much of the distribution data relied on here.

It also provided a good deal of detailed information about the morphology and ecology of area reptiles and amphibians that is beyond the scope of this work. Interest in a more thorough consideration of these aspects is best satisfied by a trip to the Canadian Museum of Nature in Aylmer, Quebec, where the data resides.

Prince Edward County reptiles and amphibians have also been the subject of several other less-intensive studies before and after the 1979 survey. These, as well as the many observations of area naturalists, are all included here to provide a picture of the status of these animals in this area.

In a final note, the many specimens of reptiles and amphibians collected in Prince Edward County during these surveys and others are available for study at several museums in Ontario or elsewhere. A list of these by species (with catalogue reference numbers) is included in Appendix C.

FROM WHENCE THIS BOOK CAME

The information about the abundance and variety of reptiles and amphibians found in Prince Edward County has been compiled here from a variety of sources.

These include the results of a survey of reptiles and amphibians completed for the County in 1979, data drawn together by Michael J. Oldham and Wayne F. Weller for the Ontario Herpetofaunal Summary, faunal information included in the Ontario Ministry of Natural Resources' wetland and watershed surveys of the area, data collected for the Long Point Bird Observatory's Marsh Monitoring Program, past information taken from the literature (in particular, a Royal Ontario Museum investigation of County wildlife published in 1941), and the personal observations of area naturalists.

Altogether, this book takes into account more than 1,000 County reptile and amphibian records compiled up to December 4, 1996. Each record indicates the observation or collection of a certain species at a specific place at a particular time. Each record may, however, account for more than one of each species seen at once at a site on that occasion. Most of the records are contemporary or recent. Others also include historic observations and other instances when specimens were collected.

The 1979 survey of amphibians and reptiles of Prince Edward County, which was conducted with considerable intensity from May 14 to September 10 of that year, provides a large share of the information relied upon here. Much of it has not been published before. The project, referred to throughout this book as the Prince Edward County Reptile and Amphibian Survey, employed naturalist Penny Briggs along with Peggy Conley, Moira Allen, Fiona Burrows, Jacqui Duyzer, Peter Christie, Eric Holmberg and Shayne Steenburgh to study the presence, abundance and natural history of reptiles and amphibians in the County.

The survey was overseen by the late W.J. Christie, formerly of the Glenora Fisheries Research Station, and Thomas A. Huff, formerly of the Reptile Breeding Foundation at Cherry Valley. Francis R. Cook, then-curator of Herpetology at the National Museum of Natural Science (now the Canadian Museum of Nature), was also instrumental in getting the survey off the ground and providing the standardized basis of data collection.

More than 300 records gathered from 190 sites sampled across Prince Edward County (and Main Duck Island) during the survey provide much of the information used in this book. Records from 28 of the total 218 sites visited by the survey team were missing from the data and could not be recovered for this volume.

Of the 190 survey sites under discussion here, 144 were visited once by the survey team. Seven particularly unique sites were revisited more than five times throughout the summer. These included: the wet pannes at the Sandbanks Provincial Park which were visited 13 times between May 17 and August 22; a beaver swamp near Yerexville (referred to throughout as the Yerexville swamp) which was visited 12 times between May 22 and August 24; a woodland stream and beaver pond on the property of W.J. Christie near Cressy (referred to throughout as Keller's Creek) which was visited eight times between June 17 and August 29; a small swamp at Green Point which was visited nine times between June 21 and August 29; a cattle pond near Hallowell (referred to here as Hallowell pond) which was visited eight times between June 21 and August 29; a man-made pond near Carrying Place (referred to here as Carrying Place pond) which was visited between June 25 and August 23; and a marsh at Little Bluff Conservation Area which was visited 10 times between July 4 and August 24.

Because of time and manpower constraints and, perhaps, because of the secretive and elusive nature of several of the animals, the findings of the 1979 survey are by no means exhaustive. The northwest of the County, namely areas around Carrying Place and Ameliasburgh, was subject to somewhat less extensive sampling than in the south and central parts of the area.

Nevertheless, and despite the years that separate its findings from this publication, the 1979 effort remains the most comprehensive investigation of Prince Edward County's reptile and amphibian fauna. Credit for compiling a good deal of the information collected after the 1979 survey goes to Michael Oldham and Wayne Weller, who have generously provided all reptile and amphibian records accumulated for Prince Edward County since they began the Ontario Herpetofaunal Summary in 1984. The results of this ongoing project are principally drawn from the observations of volunteers but also from museum records, the literature and elsewhere. The Ontario Herpetofaunal Summary adds more than 650 records to those of the 1979 survey.

The work of the Ontario Ministry of Natural Resources is another important source of the data included in this volume. Since the mid-1980s, the ministry has undertaken the task of evaluating notable wetlands in the province, applying a consistent set of criteria in an effort to evaluate their relative importance. Thirty-seven wetlands were identified within Prince Edward County. Most researchers charged with exploring these areas—in many cases more than once—included species lists of reptiles and amphibians encountered during their work. After wading through these surveys at the ministry's Kingston office, the author has summarized this information here.

The ministry was also responsible for an overview of area flora, fauna and geography, titled *An Ecological and Geological Overview of Prince Edward County*, completed in 1973 by Whitcombe et al. Surveys of two of the County's major drainage systems, one at the Consecon Creek watershed and another at the Black River drainage basin, have also been relied upon here for some faunal information.

Volunteers with the Long Point Bird Observatory's Marsh Monitoring Program also have provided records for Prince Edward County frogs and toads reported singing at area wetlands in 1995 and 1996. The program, coordinated by Amy Chabot, is a collaborative effort by the Long Point Bird Observatory,

Environment Canada and the U.S. Great Lakes Protection Fund to monitor habitat and species population changes in Ontario marshes. Much of the data is provided by volunteers visiting designated marshes and reporting the song activity of birds and amphibians.

Some additional data has been drawn from a summer-long survey of some of these animals at the Prince Edward Point National Wildlife Area conducted by Fiona Burrows in 1981.

Meanwhile, the late W.J. Christie and Thomas A. Huff are responsible for a number of the personal observations noted in this book. In particular, W.J. Christie's diaries of natural history observations around his Cressy-area home are used here to refer to the singing periods for various County frogs and toads.

Additional historical information has been primarily drawn from *A Faunal Investigation of Prince Edward County, Ontario* conducted by researchers with the Royal Ontario Museum of Zoology and published by the University of Toronto Press in 1941. The field work for this study, which includes a chapter on reptiles and amphibians written up by E.B.S. Logier, was completed from May 20 to late summer, 1930.

MORE ABOUT THIS BOOK

Descriptions and Illustrations

The descriptions and illustrations in this book are meant to provide a cursory guide to the identification of Prince Edward County reptiles and amphibians. More thorough discussions of the characteristics of identification of the animals included here are best found in the many field guides to reptiles and amphibians of the region. Similarly, keys to the identification of tadpole and other stages of life for these species may be found elsewhere.

The brief descriptions that are included here are drawn together and distilled from a variety of sources, including Conant and Collins (1991), Cook (1984), Johnson (1989) and personal observations. The maximum recorded lengths of the animals discussed here are drawn from Conant and Collins (1991) and reflect measures taken for each species throughout their eastern and central North American ranges.

The ink illustrations are likewise a product of amalgamation; a variety of photographs and drawings was used as reference while depicting these reptiles and amphibians in order to best reflect their identifying characteristics.

Species Abundance

Discussion of the relative abundance of animals is always a difficult task. Healthy populations of one species may be considerably less numerous or visible than healthy populations of another. Also, the words used to describe abundance are so frustratingly subjective they are frequently less than helpful. This book attempts to simplify these issues by limiting discussions of abundance to three categories: common, uncommon and rare. Common is meant here to refer to animals that are likely to be found during a thorough search of suitable habitat. Uncommon means a fruitful search of suitable habitat is unlikely. Rare implies that encountering an animal is improbable.

These categories may be qualified further, but attempts have been made to keep these qualifications simple: Common and widespread, for instance, suggests the animals under discussion can be found in most if not all areas of suitable habitat in Prince Edward County, usually with little effort and often in considerable numbers. Likewise, populations may be considered common and localized, meaning that the animals occur in healthy numbers only in particular localities within the County.

Additional abundance categories used here describe some species as hypothetical or extirpated. These terms refer to records of reptile and amphibians in the County that are questionable or antiquated. They mean that finding these animals on the island is very unlikely even where suitable habitat exists.

Distribution Maps

The maps accompanying the text represent sites where there are known collection or observation records for each species in Prince Edward County. These have been primarily accumulated from the Prince Edward County Reptile and Amphibian Survey, indicated with a circle. Other records come from the Ontario Herpetofaunal Summary, the Ontario Ministry of Natural Resources and elsewhere and are marked with a square. Observations drawn from literature accounts (principally the 1941 Royal Ontario Museum faunal survey) are indicated with a triangle. This difference in the demarcation illustrates pre-1979 records (triangles), 1979 records (circles) and post-1979 records (squares) and is intended to provide a rough picture of changes in the animal communities over time.

In many cases (both contemporary and historic), each of the symbols marking the distribution of species represent sites where there has been more than one observation or record of an animal or where several of a particular species have been seen at one time. In most cases, more detailed information about where and when animals were seen or collected is included in the accompanying text.

The records are located on the maps using the latitude and longitude coordinates the data provides or, in cases where these are not available, descriptions of the sites are used to determine where they are. In the case of records from the Ontario Herpetofaunal Summary, observations have been recorded based on a zone and grid system identical to that used for the *Ontario Breeding Bird Atlas* (Cadman et al. 1987). In many cases, these grid identifiers can pinpoint the location of the sighting with some accuracy. In others, the site of the observation can only be identified within a 10 km-by-10 km square, sometimes with location notes.

The distribution symbols cover a large area (approximately one square kilometre) and do not provide point-site directions for locating particular reptiles and amphibians in Prince Edward County. This is beyond the scope of this work and would not be in the interest of the animals in any case. Instead, the maps are for general reference. Researchers seeking more specific site information should contact the author.

The mapped distributions are, of course, not exclusive of any other areas where these animals may be uncovered in Prince Edward County in the future. Consequently, naturalists should not be surprised to encounter species in areas where they have not been previously observed.

Taxonomic Order and Unconfirmed Species

The taxonomic designations (common and scientific names) for species that currently occur in Prince Edward County and the order in which they are presented follow those of Conant and Collins (1991). Animals for which only one or two recent records exist in Prince Edward County or for which there are only historical or unconfirmed records are treated in a separate Unconfirmed Species section that follows discussions of reptiles and amphibians known to reside here. A section designated Other Hypothetical Species lists animals rumoured to have occurred in the area or have been found nearby.

Literature cited

Cadman, M.D., P.F.J. Eagles and F.M. Helleiner (eds.). 1987. *Atlas of Breeding Birds of Ontario.* University of Waterloo Press, Waterloo. 617 pp.

Conant, R. and J.T. Collins. 1991. *A Field Guide to Reptiles and Amphibians, Eastern and Central North America.* 3rd Ed. Houghton Mifflin Co., New York. 450 pp.

Cook, F.R. 1984. *Introduction to Canadian Amphibians and Reptiles.* Museum of Natural Sciences, Ottawa. 200 pp.

Johnson, B. 1989. *Familiar Amphibians and Reptiles of Ontario.* Natural Heritage/Natural History Inc., Toronto. 168 pp.

ABOUT PRINCE EDWARD COUNTY

Prince Edward County, parochially known as the County, was a low, irregularly shaped peninsula on the north shore of the eastern end of Lake Ontario before it was finally settled by United Empire Loyalists at the start of the nineteenth century.

The 1010-square-kilometre area, with its deep bays and varied shoreline, became a man-made island when the construction of the Murray Canal severed its narrow neck a century ago. The County's basic geological structure, according to the *Prince Edward Region Conservation Report* (1968), is a flat limestone plateau sloping gently to the south.

The bedrock was laid down as sediment while the area was covered by a Paleozoic sea and only exposes its irregular Precambrian base in a 100-metre-high granite outcrop about five kilometres northeast of Ameliasburgh. A fault line, characterized by a bluff above the west side of Picton, extends south to Point Petre. Other low bluffs expose sedimentary layers of limestone and shale throughout the County. Over distant time, the march of glaciers has stripped the County of much of its soil, leaving 60 per cent of the region with a remarkably shallow layer of earth,

Bay of Quinte — Rossmore — Massasauga Point — North Port — Green Point — Sawguin Creek — Huff's Island — Big Island — Big Island Marsh — Roblin Mills — Indian Point — Albury Swamp — Ameliasburgh — Crofton Swamp — Demorestville — Frinyer's Cove — Roblin Lake — Carrying Place — Allisonville — Big Swamp — Lost Lake — Keller's Creek — Cressy — Picton — Lake-On-The-Mountain — Waupoos — Wellers Bay — Consecon — Hillier — Bloomfield — Smith Bay — Pleasant Bay — Wellington — Beaver Meadow — Black River — Morrison Point — Huycks Bay — Garret Island — Milford — Little Bluff — Prince Edward Point — West Lake — East Lake — Cherry Valley — South Bay — Lake Ontario — Sandbanks — Outlet — Petticoat Point — Salmon Point — Soup Harbour — Point Petre

Prince Edward County

frequently less than 75 centimetres deep. Organic soils occupy just 10 per cent of the area, while clay, sand and sandy loams cover a further 16 per cent.

A fan-shaped sand plain south and west of Picton reaches toward East and West Lake and covers the bedrock with depths of up to 23 metres. The *Conservation Report* also characterizes the northern foot of the County plateau and the shoreline there as clay plain. Notable features include three inland lakes along the top rim of the limestone plateau—Fish Lake, Roblin Lake and Lake-On-The-Mountain—as well as the extensive sand dunes and pannes of the Sandbanks Provincial Park that stretch northwest to southeast to form the western perimeter of East and West Lake.

Much of the County is covered by active farmland, abandoned pastures and small to extensive woodlots. Wetlands, a principal habitat for many reptile and amphibian species, also cover relatively significant areas of Prince Edward County, despite well-documented shrinkage of Bay of Quinte marshes over the past half-century. County wetlands were estimated by Crowder et al (1986) to occupy some 4074 hectares (or some 4 per cent of the total area) based on surveys done in 1979. A look at historic surveys suggest wetlands were 8-to-10 per cent larger in 1929, despite higher water levels at the time. The largest of four County watershed systems identified by the authors of the *Prince Edward Region Conservation Report* is the Consecon Creek watershed which has a drainage area of some 190 square kilometres. The system starts near Roblin Mills south of Fish Lake and runs west to Wellers Bay, essentially bisecting the northern half of the County. The 23-km-long main creek bed of this system passes through the significant wooded wetland, known as the Big Swamp. The northeast drainage system runs from near Green Point west to Fish Lake and Demorestville Creek through to Muscote Bay. The 10-km-long system is particularly boggy where the creek leaves Fish Lake. The lower plateau east of Glenora is drained by a number of small streams running down either side of the Cressy point. The final watershed, the lowland watershed system runs between Carrying Place and Muscote Bay and is drained by the 19-km-long Sawguin Creek. The marsh along the south and west perimeter of Big Island and Muscote Bay is by far the County's largest. Other significant marshes are found at Lost Lake, Fish Lake, West Lake, East Lake, Soup Harbour, South Bay, Smith Bay, Black River and along the Long Point peninsula.

MacDonald (1987) lists sugar maple, red and bur oak, beech, basswood, red and white ash, shagbark hickory, ironwood and yellow birch as species characterizing many hardwood stands in the area. White pine, eastern hemlock and balsam fir are also frequently found mixed in. Other common tree species include bigtooth aspen, black cherry and butternut. Red cedar is ubiquitous in dry, upland areas with shallow soil and abandoned pastures. The latter also frequently hosts sumac, prickly ash, hawthorn and apple. Wetter, lowland areas are often characterized by the presence of eastern white cedar, silver maple, red elm, black ash, willow, dogwood and alder.

This book also includes information about the reptiles and amphibians of Main Duck Island which lies near the middle of Lake Ontario, 19 km southeast of Prince Edward Point.

Literature cited

Crowder, A.A., B. McLaughlin, R.D. Weir and W.J. Christie. 1986. Shoreline Fauna of the Bay of Quinte. p. 190-200. In C. K. Minns, D. A. Hurley and K. H. Nicholls [eds.] *Project Quinte: Point-Source Phosphorous Control and Ecosystem Response in the Bay of Quinte, Lake Ontario.* Can. Spec. Publ. Fish. Aquat. Sci. 86: 270 pp.

MacDonald, I.D. 1987. *Life Science Areas of Natural and Scientific Interest in Site District 6-5.* Parks and Recreation Areas Section, Ontario Ministry of Natural Resources, Eastern Region, Kemptville. 149 pp.

Prince Edward Region Conservation Authority. 1968. *Prince Edward Region Conservation Report.* Conservation Authorities Branch, Department of Energy and Resources Management, Toronto. 161 pp.

Description

This prehistoric-looking reptile is the largest turtle in Prince Edward County, with adult shells measuring up to 49.4 cm. Dark brown to black, the Common Snapping Turtle is easily recognized by its large head, its rough, often algae-covered shell and its long tail topped with tooth-like scales. These turtles are known for their short temper when encountered on land. The Snapping Turtle is most often found in large streams or any permanent body of water, frequently preferring those with a muddy bottom.

Distribution

The Common Snapping Turtle is common and widespread in Prince Edward County and can often be seen bobbing like a log offshore or patrolling the shallows of ponds and lakes.

The Prince Edward County Reptile and Amphibian Survey encountered the Snapping Turtle in many of the County's inland lakes, including Lake Consecon, Fish Lake, West Lake, East Lake and the land-locked bays of Pleasant Bay and Huycks Bay. Lake-On-The-Mountain and Roblin Lake were the exceptions, with no Snapping Turtles found in the limited sampling done in those areas. The Snapping Turtle was also uncovered during hoopnet and dipnet trapping in the County's larger streams, rivers and permanent ponds situated adjacent to the Lake Ontario shoreline (ie. Prince Edward Point, Little Bluff Conservation Area and near Indian Point). Along a five-kilometre stretch of Black River between Milford and Prince Edward Bay, three individuals of this impressive reptile were discovered in a single afternoon.

Altogether the survey team reported 18 records for the Snapping Turtle at 16 of 190 sites visited. Despite local observations that the Snapping Turtle population in the County was under considerable pressure from commercial harvesting in 1979, the report of the Reptile and Amphibian Survey concludes that the species is "quite common" throughout the larger bodies of water in the area.

The Ontario Herpetofaunal Summary adds 21 records for the Snapping Turtle in the County since the Reptile and Amphibian Survey. They describe the Snapping Turtle making an appearance on land, crossing roads or seeking suitable nesting sites near Allisonville, Ameliasburgh, Big Swamp, the Outlet, Huffs Island and South Bay.

In its series of surveys of Prince Edward County wetlands, the Ontario Ministry of Natural Resources discovered the Common Snapping Turtle during 13 of the 21 surveys that included faunal lists between 1984 and 1993. These represented sites distributed throughout the County, including swamps near Ameliasburgh, Crofton Swamp, Big Island Marsh, Cressy, Huycks Bay, East Lake, West Lake, Sawguin Creek, Fish Lake and Wellers Bay. The Snapping Turtle is also mentioned in the ministry's 1973 *Ecological and Geological Overview of Prince Edward County* as well as its 1975 watershed survey of the Consecon Creek drainage basin and in its 1976 watershed survey of the Black River system. Researchers with the Royal Ontario Museum's 1941 *Faunal Investigation of Prince Edward County, Ontario* collected one Snapping Turtle specimen in Hallowell Township with a shell measuring 28 cm. Two turtle nests were also found in Hallowell. Otherwise, reports of the Snapping Turtle at the time were scant, leading authors to conclude the animal "must be commoner than our records would indicate."

Despite its apparently healthy numbers in Prince Edward County today, the future of the Snapping Turtle in the area and throughout Ontario may be in some danger; it continues to suffer through annual summer-long harvests by fishermen interested in its meat. While commercial fishing for the turtles was outlawed a few years ago, residents and non-residents alike are still permitted to take two turtles a day during a two-month season in this area. (They may possess a maximum of five at any time.) Todd Norris, district ecologist with the Ontario Ministry of Natural Resources, notes that it has become common for Americans to visit the province for the express purpose of stalking turtles, although the specific numbers of turtles taken is unknown. For this slow-to-mature species, a growing harvest may yet have serious consequences for Snapping Turtle populations in Prince Edward County.

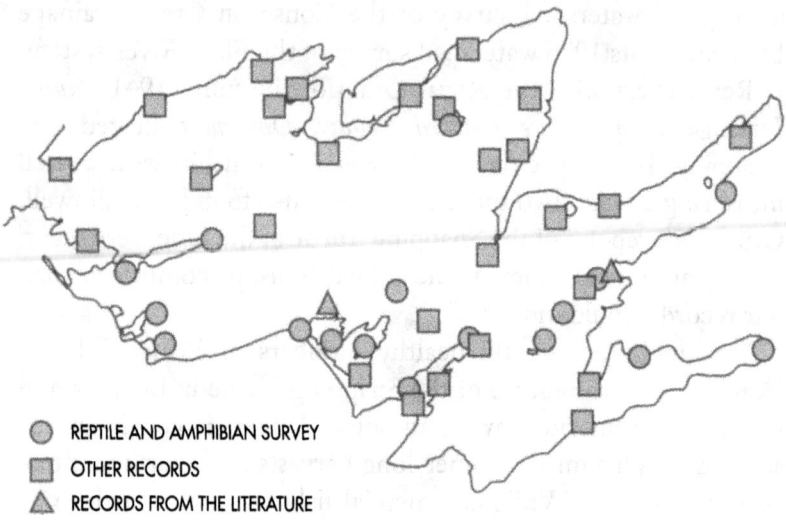

○ REPTILE AND AMPHIBIAN SURVEY
■ OTHER RECORDS
▲ RECORDS FROM THE LITERATURE

Common Musk Turtle
Sternotherus odoratus

Description

This elusive, bottom-dwelling species is Prince Edward County's smallest turtle, with a shell length not larger than 13.7 cm.

The Common Musk Turtle is recognized by its high-domed, often algae-covered shell and the two light stripes along the side of its head. The Stinkpot, as the Musk Turtle is otherwise known, is dark and most easily distinguished from the Common Snapping Turtle (*Chelydra serpentina serpentina*) by its much shorter tail, lacking any tooth-like scales on the top. Captured or frightened, these turtles frequently exude a musky odour. The Stinkpot is most often found in established and permanent ponds and lakes, but the turtle's dark appearance and habit of foraging on the bottom make encountering one unlikely.

Distribution

The Common Musk Turtle is uncommon in Prince Edward County, but its secretive, aquatic habits makes any estimation of the abundance of this species in the area speculative.

In searches of the area's lakes and ponds, the Prince Edward County Reptile and Amphibian Survey team uncovered only two individual Musk Turtles and the shell remains of another at three of 190 sites sampled. The two live turtles were captured during hoopnet trapping, one in the west-end marsh of East Lake and the other in a marsh along the south shore of West Lake. The shell remains of a third specimen were discovered on West Lake's Garrett Island. The survey's report is inconclusive about the abundance of the Stinkpot in Prince Edward County, suggesting the survey team's sampling methods may simply have been inappropriate for trapping this somewhat elusive turtle.

The Ontario Herpetofaunal Summary includes six additional records for the Stinkpot since the Reptile and Amphibian Survey. Most of these were reported in and around East Lake and West Lake. The most recent record, a young turtle found on July 7, 1990, was reported at the Outlet. Thomas Huff of the Reptile Breeding Foundation at Cherry Valley reported finding Stinkpots in the spring of 1987 near East Lake, near Prince Edward Point and at Lost Lake in Cressy. The Ontario Ministry of Natural Resources, meanwhile, includes a record for the Stinkpot in its 1973 *Ecological and Geological Overview of Prince Edward County*.

Five Musk Turtle records were reported in the Royal Ontario Museum's 1941 *Faunal Investigation of Prince Edward County, Ontario*. Three of these were of specimens collected near Wellington in 1936. All were females, measuring 9, 11.5 and 13 cm in shell length. A fourth was sighted by area resident W.J. LeRay at Prinyer's Cove in North Marysburgh, and the shell remains of another was discovered in the same area.

○ REPTILE AND AMPHIBIAN SURVEY
▢ OTHER RECORDS
▲ RECORDS FROM THE LITERATURE

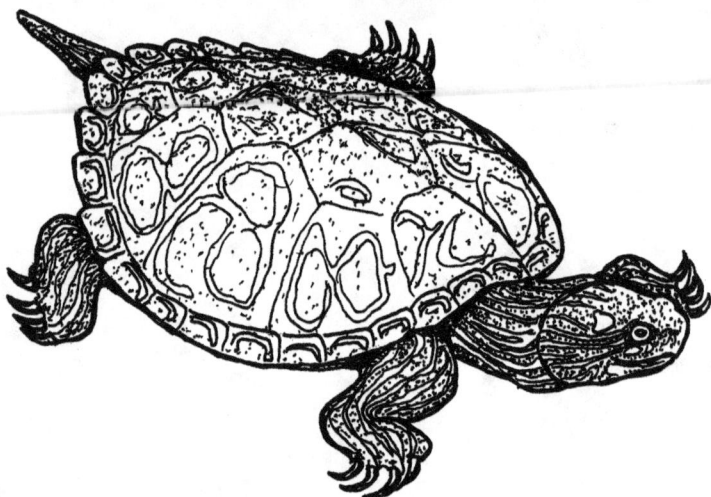

Description

This medium-sized turtle (up to 27.3 cm) is among Prince Edward County's notably shy reptiles.

The Common Map Turtle is recognized by the light, irregular, yellowish markings which can be thought of as resembling a map on its brown shell. The legs, neck and head are marked by yellow lines. The rear edge of the shell is serrated unlike that of the Painted Turtle which is smooth. This turtle is most frequently spotted basking on logs and rocks that break the surface of the rivers, lakes and large, open ponds it calls home. However, the Map Turtle's skittish nature often means it is scrambling back into the water well ahead of any close approach.

Distribution

Often quick to disappear from view, the Common Map Turtle is nevertheless common in Prince Edward County but with localized populations.

The Prince Edward County Reptile and Amphibian Survey reported 11 Common Map Turtle records at just four of 190 sites sampled. Two additional sites at Baker Island and Hay Bay off the County's shores in the Bay of Quinte where Map Turtles were captured were included in the survey data. The others were caught in hoopnet sampling at Picton, Cressy and East Lake. One, a female, was found on land near West Lake, likely returning to the water after nesting. The survey concludes in its report that the Map Turtle population in Prince Edward County was largely along the Bay of Quinte/Lake Ontario shoreline on the island's periphery.

The Ontario Herpetofaunal Survey describes 13 additional records of the Common Map Turtle in the County since the Reptile and Amphibian Survey. The majority of the Map Turtle observations reported these turtles basking along the shores of East and West Lake or nesting nearby.

The Ontario Ministry of Natural Resources included records for the Common Map Turtle in its surveys of wetlands near Carrying Place (July 1984), the east end of East Lake (August 1991), near Massasauga Point (August 1990, July 1993), and Sawguin Creek Marsh (August 1993). Ministry researchers also reported Map Turtles in their drainage system survey of Black River in 1976 and mention the species in its 1973 *Ecological and Geological Overview of Prince Edward County*.

The 1941 *Faunal Investigation of Prince Edward County, Ontario* reported that the Royal Ontario Museum researchers in that study found no sign of the Common Map Turtle in the County during their field work in 1930. Instead, the survey summary refers only to two museum specimens collected from some unspecified place in the Bay of Quinte in 1927. The report also mentions the observations of area resident W.J. LeRay who reported occasionally seeing the Map Turtle at Prinyer's Cove in North Marysburgh in 1938 and 1939.

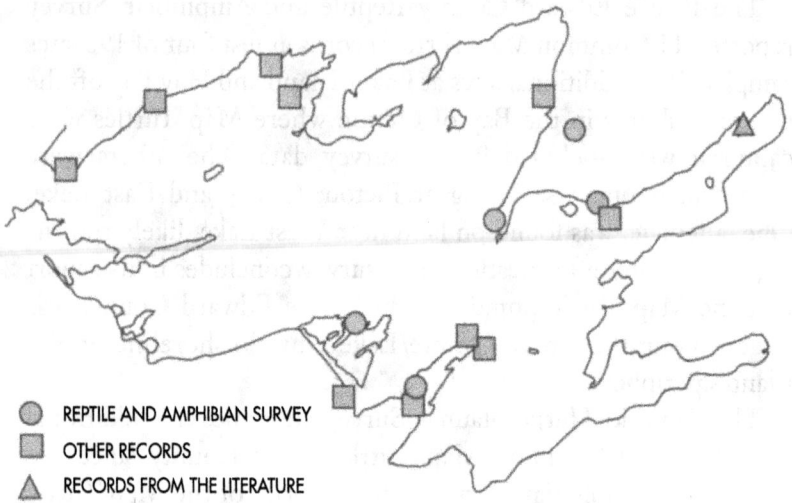

REPTILE AND AMPHIBIAN SURVEY
OTHER RECORDS
RECORDS FROM THE LITERATURE

Midland Painted Turtle
Chrysemys picta marginata

Description

This attractive, medium-sized (up to 18.1 cm) turtle is a dependable resident of Prince Edward County ponds and rivers.

The Midland Painted Turtle is easily recognized by its smooth olive-green shell with red designs adorning the edges. Its head, legs and tail also show distinctive yellow and red markings. A large, dark blotch usually marks the centre of its belly plate. The Painted Turtle is most often found in shallow bodies of water such as ponds, marshes, streams and lakes, preferring those with an abundance of vegetation and a muddy bottom. It is a common sight basking on shoreline logs and rocks.

Distribution

Midland Painted Turtles are common and widespread throughout Prince Edward County wherever suitable ponds, marshes and rivers are found.

The Prince Edward County Reptile and Amphibian Survey found populations of the Painted Turtle in all sites with suitable habitat, including ponds, marshes along the area's major streams or the swampy margins of local lakes and bays. Altogether, the survey team reported 38 records of the Painted Turtle at 31 of 190 sites sampled through the summer. In some of these localities, the turtle populations were surprisingly dense. For instance, survey researchers paddling a canoe along five kilometres of Black River from Milford to near Prince Edward Bay counted 178 Painted Turtles slipping from floating logs into the water ahead of them or swimming nearby.

The Ontario Herpetofaunal Summary includes 33 records for the Midland Painted Turtle in the County since the Reptile and Amphibian Survey, as well as three others from the early 1970s. The distribution of these records confirm that this species is ubiquitous, preferring murky, marshy ponds and streams to the open water of Lake Ontario and the Bay of Quinte on the County's periphery.

The Ontario Ministry of Natural Resources' surveys of area wetlands discovered the Midland Painted Turtle at 14 of the 21 sites that included any faunal lists. These were spread evenly throughout the County, supporting other evidence that the species is widespread and abundant throughout the island. Reference to the species is also included in the ministry's 1973 *Ecological and Geological Overview of Prince Edward County* and is mentioned in the ministry's 1976 watershed survey of the Black River drainage system.

Researchers with the Royal Ontario Museum's 1941 *Faunal Investigation of Prince Edward County, Ontario* reported collecting 18 specimens, all female, of the Midland Painted Turtle around West Lake and Wellington during their field work in 1930. The largest of the group had a shell measuring 16.5 cm. They also note the observations of area resident W.J. LeRay who also found the turtle at Prinyer's Cove. The report of the investigation concludes that "there is no reason to doubt that (the Midland Painted Turtle) is common all over the County where suitable situations occur."

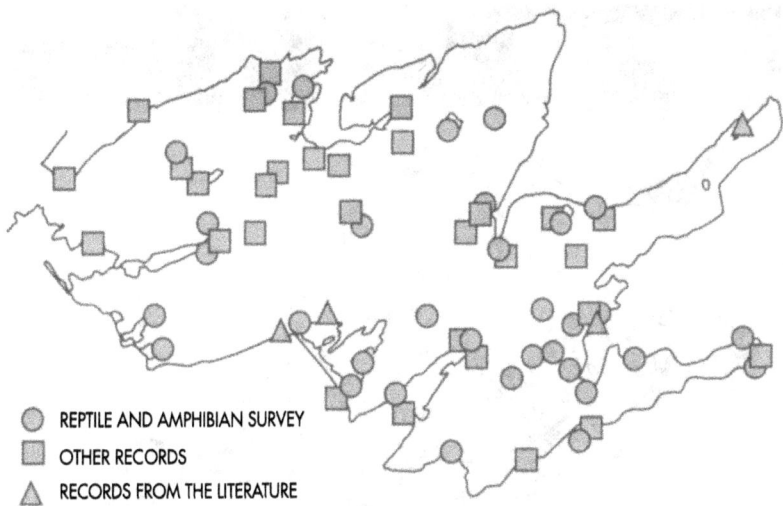

REPTILE AND AMPHIBIAN SURVEY
OTHER RECORDS
RECORDS FROM THE LITERATURE

Blanding's Turtle
Emydoidea blandingii

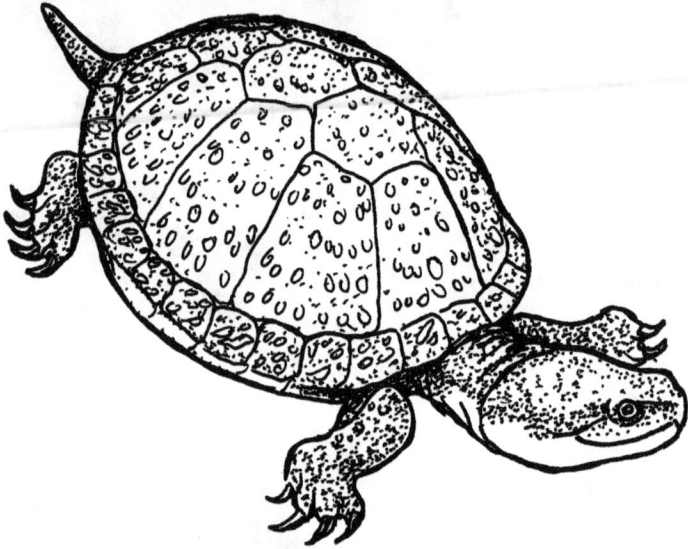

Description

The bright, yellow throat of this large (shell length up to 27.4 cm) turtle readily distinguishes it from other Prince Edward County species.

Otherwise, the Blanding's Turtle is characterized by a dark head and high-domed grey-to-black shell which is covered with light spots. Field guides often refer to the hinge across its belly that enables it to tuck its legs and neck up tightly under its shell, a characteristic that has earned it the name semi-box turtle. The Blanding's Turtle prefers marshes, bogs, ponds and lakes where it can often be seen bobbing leisurely at the water's surface or basking on waterside logs and rocks.

Distribution

The Blanding's Turtle is common in Prince Edward County, but it is abundant only in localized populations.

The Prince Edward County Reptile and Amphibian Survey discovered the Blanding's Turtle in healthy numbers in stream mouths and lake-end marshes in much of the County. The survey reported 12 records for the Blanding's Turtle at 12 of 190 sites sampled. These were distributed throughout the area, but two sites revealed populations that were considerably more dense than others. In particular, Fish Lake's shallow water and reedy shoreline seemed to provide an ideal habitat for Blanding's Turtles. The survey team encountered extraordinary numbers of the turtles there, swimming or basking on waterside logs and rocks (about 20 during a single visit). The density of the Blanding's Turtle population at Soup Harbour, a bay of limestone beaches and a marshy stream outlet, of 12 during one visit was similarly surprising. The survey's report concludes that the Blanding's Turtle which has a spotty distribution in its range east of Ontario was "doing well" in Prince Edward County.

The Ontario Herpetofaunal Summary has compiled 35 additional records for the Blanding's Turtle for the County since the Reptile and Amphibian Survey. These are predominantly from the south and east of the County, especially near Prince Edward Point, near Demorestville and at East Lake.

The Ontario Ministry of Natural Resources' surveys of area wetlands uncovered Blanding's Turtle at the Big Island Marsh (August 1993), East Lake (August 1991), Lake-On-The-Mountain (July 1993), Lake Consecon (August 1986), near Muscote Bay (August 1992) and near Petticoat Point (August 1993). The Blanding's Turtle is also mentioned in the ministry's 1973 *Ecological and Geological Overview of Prince Edward County* and was reported at Black River in the ministry's 1976 watershed survey there.

The 1941 Royal Ontario Museum's *Faunal Investigation of Prince Edward County, Ontario* reported collecting Blanding's Turtle specimens from near Waupoos in 1928 and another from the Big Swamp area in 1930. The report also mentions a Blanding's Turtle spotted at Big Island in 1930 and others seen by area resident W.J. LeRay at Prinyer's Cove in 1938 and 1939.

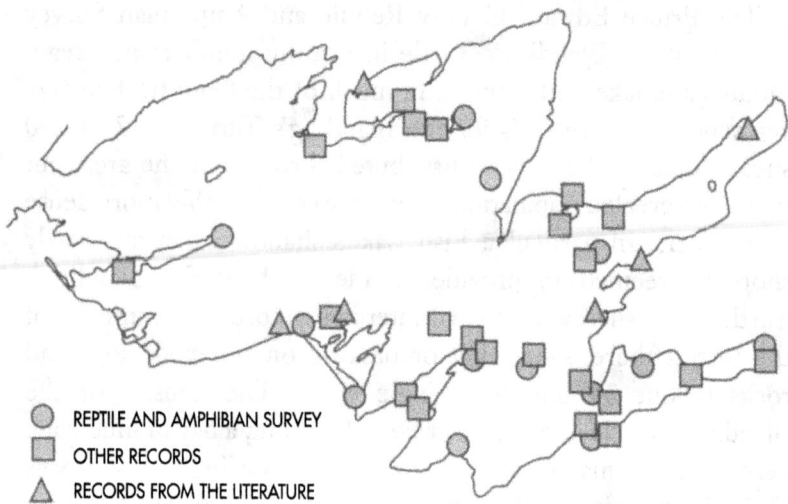

REPTILE AND AMPHIBIAN SURVEY
OTHER RECORDS
RECORDS FROM THE LITERATURE

SNAKES
Northern Water Snake
Nerodia sipedon sipedon

Description

This aquatic serpent is the largest snake currently found in Prince Edward County (up to 140.5 cm long).

Dark brown to grey, the Northern Water Snake is best recognized by the pattern of saddle-like, brown blotches on its back. These are obscured on some large adults which may appear to be uniformly dark brown or black. Older snakes often have distinctly thick bodies. Northern Water Snakes prefer streams, ponds, lakes and other permanent bodies of water where they can frequently be seen basking on waterside logs and branches. When cornered or handled, these snakes are known to show their cantankerous side.

Distribution

The Northern Water Snake is common and widespread in and around Prince Edward County's marshy shores and ponds and on Main Duck Island.

The Prince Edward County Reptile and Amphibian Survey found the Northern Water Snake in many areas with suitable habitat sampled on the eastern side of the County, including the

Big Island Marsh, Fish Lake, the Bay of Quinte, Picton, Lake-On-The-Mountain, Lost Lake, Black River, Little Bluff, Prince Edward Point and a small number of inland swamps. Altogether, the survey reported 29 records for the Northern Water Snake at 14 of 190 sites sampled. These were principally in the eastern half of the County where limestone outcrops characterize the shoreline.

Two sites sampled by the survey team were remarkable for their extraordinary densities of Northern Water Snakes. The limestone bluffs and shingle beaches of Main Duck Island revealed surprising numbers of these snakes (more than 100 in two days of sampling)—often several under a single turned stone. This large population was also mixed with a large number of Eastern Garter Snakes (*Thamnophis sirtalis sirtalis*) at a ratio of approximately two Water Snakes to one Garter Snake. Another dense population of large Northern Water Snakes inhabited a shallow, forested swamp some distance south of Fish Lake. The records of three visits to the site describe seeing more than 30 snakes at one time. The size of these snakes was as remarkable as their numbers; most measured more than a meter and the longest measured 121 cm.

The Ontario Herpetofaunal Summary adds 35 records of the Northern Water Snake found in the County since the Reptile and Amphibian Survey. Again, the majority of these are from sites located on the eastern side of the County with four from the sandy areas along the shores of East and West lakes.

Researchers participating in the Ontario Ministry of Natural Resources' surveys of area wetlands reported finding the Northern Water Snake at Ameliasburgh (August 1993), East Lake (August 1991), Lake-On-The-Mountain (July 1993), Sawguin Creek (August 1993) and Wellers Bay (August 1993). Northern Water Snakes are also mentioned in the ministry's 1973 *Ecological and Geological Overview of Prince Edward County* and its watershed survey of the Black River drainage system completed in 1976.

Researchers with the 1941 *Faunal Investigation of Prince Edward County, Ontario* reported collecting only one Northern

Water Snake specimen, measuring 91 cm, from the Cressy area in 1930. Another was spotted near Hallowell. The survey notes area resident W.J. LeRay's observation that the snake was "common" in Cressy in 1938 and 1939 and another 1937 report by letter from local resident Grant Carman that it was "decreasing generally." The report concludes that the Northern Water Snake was "conspicuous by its absence in various likely-looking places where one would have expected to have found it."

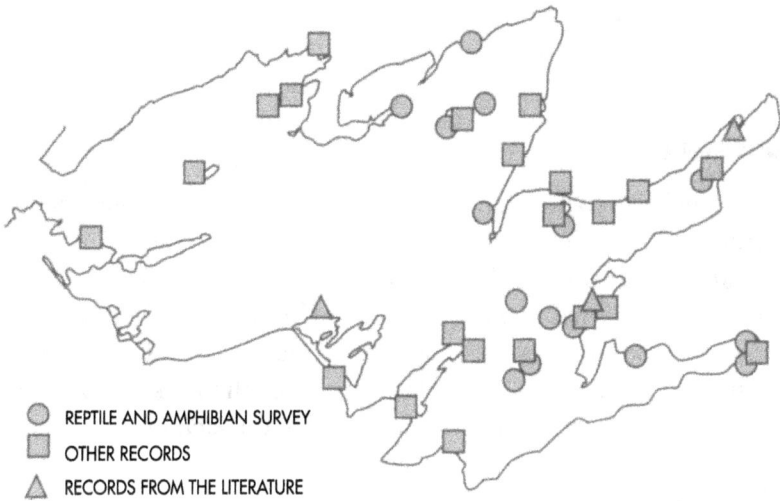

○ REPTILE AND AMPHIBIAN SURVEY
□ OTHER RECORDS
△ RECORDS FROM THE LITERATURE

Brown Snake
Storeria dekayi

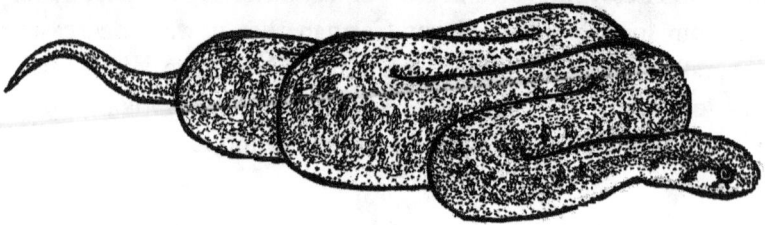

Description

This small (up to 49.2 cm) snake may be most remarkable among Prince Edward County snakes for its plain appearance.

Tan to dark brown, the Brown Snake (formerly known as the DeKay's Snake) has two parallel rows of black spots down its back (Francis Cook points out that some variants—mainly in southwestern Ontario—may have dark bars over the back joining the spots). A conspicuous dark mark is visible on each of the snake's temples. Often found hiding under old boards and logs, the Brown Snake prefers woods, old meadows or abandoned lots.

Distribution

The Brown Snake is uncommon in Prince Edward County, but its secretive habits may make this designation more apparent than real.

The Prince Edward County Reptile and Amphibian Survey uncovered few Brown Snakes. A dozen of the snakes were found at four of 190 sites sampled by the survey crew. These were all in the southern half of the County. The largest concentration of the snake was encountered along the shingle beach at Little Bluff. There, six of the species were found under broad flat limestone rocks and boards over two visits. Others were found in drier, upland areas under boards and logs and on roads after being killed by cars. The project's report concludes that the species "should be more common than this survey indicates" and adds that the small number of suitable sites sampled may have contributed to this shortcoming.

The Ontario Herpetofaunal Summary adds 17 records for the Brown Snake in Prince Edward County. These are again concentrated in the south and east of the area and were found under logs and boards or, frequently, dead on roads near suitable habitat.

A Brown Snake record is included in the Ontario Ministry of Natural Resources' wetland survey of the marsh at Ameliasburgh (August 1993). Mention of the species is also included in the ministry's 1973 *Ecological and Geological Overview of Prince Edward County* and in its watershed survey of the Black River drainage system completed in 1976.

The 1941 *Faunal Investigation of Prince Edward County, Ontario* describes collecting two specimens of the Brown Snake at Garrett Island in West Lake and at East Lake in 1930. The survey also mentions observations of the snake by area resident W.J. LeRay who reported finding the snake near Cressy in 1938 and 1939 "but not commonly."

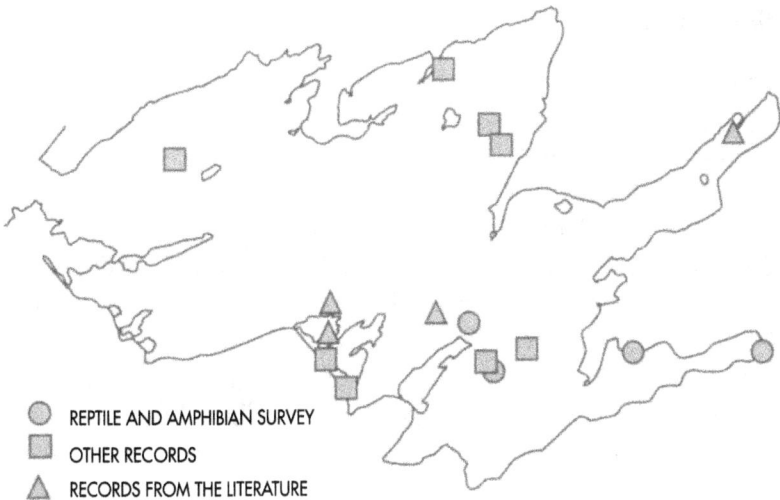

○ REPTILE AND AMPHIBIAN SURVEY
▣ OTHER RECORDS
△ RECORDS FROM THE LITERATURE

Northern Redbelly Snake
Storeria occipitomaculata occipitomaculata

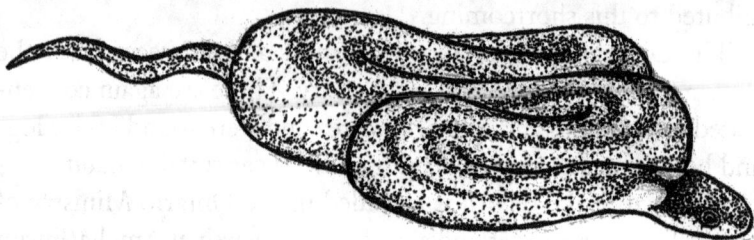

Description

This small (up to 40.6 cm long), attractive snake is among Prince Edward County's most delicate reptiles.

The Northern Redbelly Snake is characterized by its distinctive orange-red belly. Otherwise, the Redbelly Snake's plain grey to reddish-brown back is interrupted only by light blotches at its neck and by small dark markings along its length. This elusive snake is most frequently found under woodland logs and rocks.

Distribution

The Northern Redbelly Snake is uncommon in Prince Edward County, although its hidden ways contribute significantly to its infrequent appearance.

The Prince Edward County Reptile and Amphibian Survey found just two Northern Redbelly Snakes at two of 190 sites sampled. Both were uncovered by rolling rotted logs at the edge of small woodlots near Prince Edward Point and near Cressy. The project's report concludes that the species "should be more common than this survey indicates" and adds that the small number of suitable sites sampled may have contributed to this shortcoming. The particularly elusive nature of these secretive snakes was certainly another likely factor.

The Ontario Herpetofaunal Summary adds another five records for the Northern Redbelly Snake since the Reptile and Amphibian Survey. Three of these were reported by Thomas Huff in 1987 in the vicinity of Milford and Cherry Valley. Another was found at the Sandbanks, and still another was discovered at Prince Edward Point. In her 1981 survey of the Prince Edward Point National Wildlife Area, Fiona Burrows also discovered a Redbelly Snake on the shingle beach near the point's lighthouse.

The Northern Redbelly Snake also makes an appearance in the Ontario Ministry of Natural Resources' wetland survey of Black River (1993), although this may have been an older record contributed to the surveyors by Thomas Huff of the Reptile Breeding Foundation. The ministry also includes the species in its list of reptiles included in its 1973 *Ecological and Geological Overview of Prince Edward County*.

The Royal Ontario Museum researchers who conducted the 1941 *Faunal Investigation of Prince Edward County, Ontario* uncovered no Redbelly Snakes in their 1930 travels of the area. The report mentions a 1937 letter from area resident Grant Carman describing a "hill black snake" that was "very black above, brilliant red beneath" and concludes that the reference could not be to any other snake than the Redbelly Snake. On the other hand, subsequent Prince Edward County records for the Northern Ringneck Snake (*Diadophis punctatus edwardsii*), whose belly can be distinctly reddish-orange, make this inference less than assured. The Royal Ontario Museum report also says area resident W.J. LeRay reported finding the Northern Redbelly Snake "occasionally" at Cressy in 1938 and 1939.

○ REPTILE AND AMPHIBIAN SURVEY
□ OTHER RECORDS
△ RECORDS FROM THE LITERATURE

Eastern Garter Snake
Thamnophis sirtalis sirtalis

Description

This ubiquitous, medium-sized-to-large (up to 123.8 cm) snake is one of Prince Edward County's most highly visible and familiar reptiles.

The Eastern Garter Snake is best recognized by the yellow stripe running down its black back and two yellow stripes running down either side. The snake's belly is pale green or yellow. The slender Northern Ribbon Snake (*Thamnophis sauritus septentrionalis*) appears to be somewhat similarly marked, but the Garter Snake is a heavier snake without the remarkably long tail that distinguishes the much-less-common Ribbon Snake.

The Eastern Garter Snake seems to make itself at home in the County in almost every variety of habitat, including marshes, fields, ravines, ditches, and vacant lots and parks.

Distribution

The Eastern Garter Snake is common and widespread throughout Prince Edward County and on Main Duck Island. But historic records suggest it may have been less abundant in the past.

The Prince Edward County Reptile and Amphibian Survey recorded observations of the Eastern Garter Snake almost uniformly dispersed across the area. The survey crew reported 38 records (often including many snakes seen at once) at 27 of 190 sites sampled (that is, most of the non-aquatic sites visited across the County). The survey found an exceptionally vigorous population of Garter Snakes on Main Duck Island. There some 50 of the snakes were found during two days of sampling along the limestone bluffs and shingle beaches ringing the shores of the island. These were mixed with a population of twice the number of Northern Water Snakes (*Nerodia sipedon sipedon*). The survey's report concludes that Eastern Garter Snakes are "widely dispersed throughout the County in a wide range of habitats."

The Ontario Herpetofaunal Summary has compiled 41 additional records for the Eastern Garter Snake in Prince Edward County since the Reptile and Amphibian Survey, including one for an all-black (melanistic) specimen collected by Thomas A. Huff at Milford in 1985. These records are, again, uniformly scattered across the island.

Records for the Eastern Garter Snake are also included in the series of area wetland surveys completed by the Ontario Ministry of Natural Resources between 1984 and 1993. Of the 21 surveys that included faunal lists, the Garter Snake was included in 10. These were widespread throughout the island. Mention of the species was included in the ministry's 1973 *Ecological and Geological Overview of Prince Edward County*. The Garter Snake was also found near Consecon Creek in the ministry's 1975 survey of that watershed and near Black River in the government's 1976 survey of the Black River drainage basin. The Eastern Garter Snake was frequently encountered by Fiona Burrows in her 1981 reptile and amphibian research at the Prince Edward Point National Wildlife Area.

Researchers with the Royal Ontario Museum's 1941 *Faunal Investigation of Prince Edward County, Ontario* describe the Eastern Garter Snake in a way that suggests it may not have been as common in 1930 as it is today. They collected 14 Garter Snakes (seven of each sex) near Hallowell, West Lake, Lake-On-The-Mountain and Waupoos. The report also mentions the 1939 observation of area resident W.J. LeRay that the snake was "fairly common" in the Cressy area. The investigation concludes that the Eastern Garter Snake "was the commonest snake although not apparently abundant."

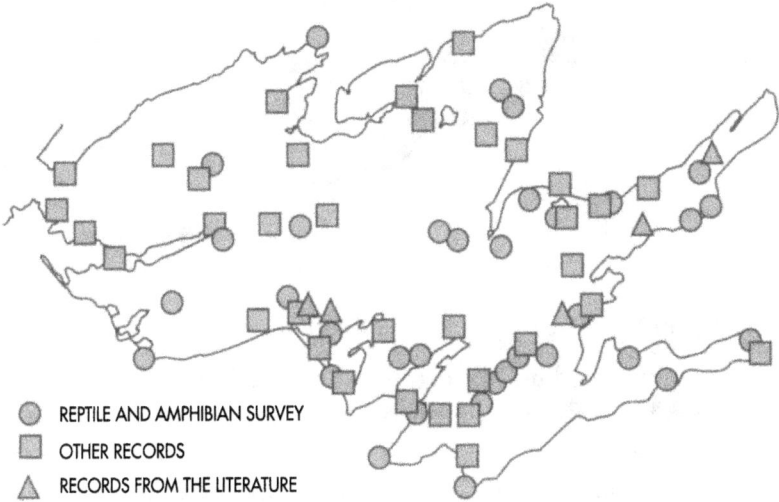

REPTILE AND AMPHIBIAN SURVEY
OTHER RECORDS
RECORDS FROM THE LITERATURE

Northern Ringneck Snake
Diadophis punctatus edwardsii

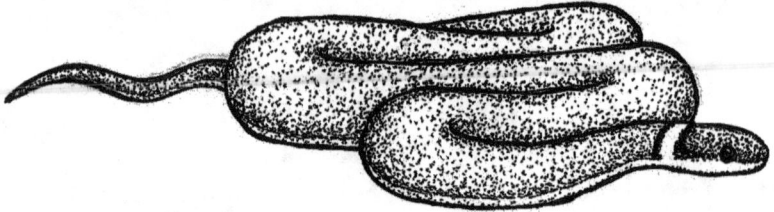

Description

This slender, medium-sized (up to 70.6 cm) species is one of Prince Edward County's most beautiful snakes and among the most elusive.

The Northern Ringneck Snake is best recognized by its attractive smooth bluish-grey back and its distinctive yellowish or orange collar. The Northern Ringneck Snake's belly, like its neck marking, is a uniform yellow or orange. Unlike most Prince Edward County snakes, the Ringneck Snake's scales are smooth, giving it a particularly sleek appearance. The ringneck snake's secretive and nocturnal habits make encountering one exceptional. It is most frequently found under bark pieces, logs and rocks on wooded hillsides or on the edges of woodland marshes.

Distribution

The Northern Ringneck Snake is rare in Prince Edward County and records of it in the area are scant.

The Prince Edward County Reptile and Amphibian Survey uncovered a single Northern Ringneck Snake under leaf litter on a hill close to the edge of Lost Lake at Cressy. The large (47.9 cm), male snake was bluish grey with a distinctly red-orange collar ring and belly. The survey's report notes earlier reports of the Ringneck Snake by area naturalists, but these were at least a decade old. Margaret Moore of the Reptile Breeding Foundation remembered seeing the snakes periodically on her farm near Morrison Point at Prince Edward Bay. Similarly, W.J. Christie recalled finding the occasional Northern Ringneck Snake inside the old mill that housed the Glenora Fisheries Research Station at Glenora (the building has since been significantly renovated).

The Ontario Herpetofaunal Summary adds three other County records for the Northern Ringneck Snake since the Reptile and Amphibian Survey. These include two observations in the spring of 1987 by Thomas A. Huff near the Sandbanks Park and near Cherry Valley. Shayne Steenburgh collected another Ringneck Snake at the entrance to the Outlet Park in June 1983.

The Northern Ringneck Snake is noticeably absent from literature references to Prince Edward County reptiles, including the Ontario Ministry of Natural Resources' 1973 *Ecological and Geological Overview of Prince Edward County*.

It is similarly absent in the Royal Ontario Museum's *Faunal Investigation of Prince Edward County, Ontario* of 1941. Interestingly, the survey's report includes in its discussion of the Northern Redbelly Snake (*Storeria occipitomaculata occipitomaculata*) a reference to a 1937 letter from local resident Grant Carman that could be describing a Northern Ringneck Snake. The letter mentions a "Hill Black Snake" that was "about 18 inches long—very black above, brilliant red beneath." The report concludes the "reference could not be to any other snake" than the Redbelly Snake. But the length described (about 45 cm) is very large for a Redbelly Snake (record length: 40.6 cm). Further, the first Northern Ringneck Snake found in the County by the 1979 survey team had a bright orange-salmon colour on its belly instead of the usual yellow.

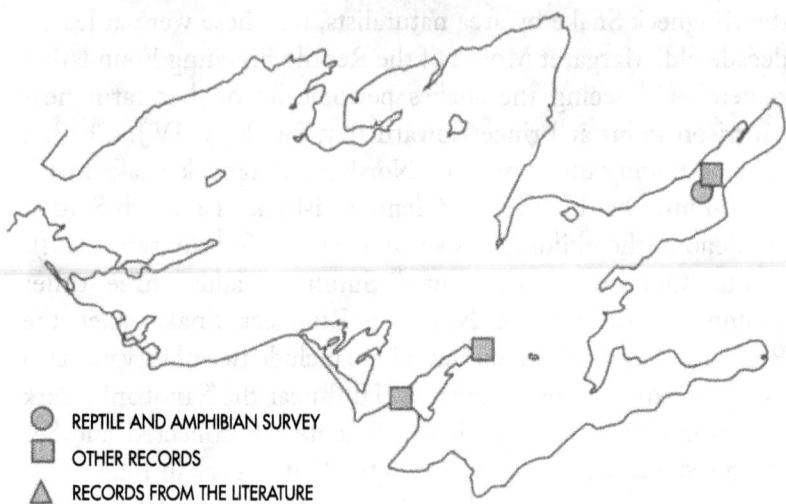

REPTILE AND AMPHIBIAN SURVEY
OTHER RECORDS
RECORDS FROM THE LITERATURE

Smooth Green Snake
Opheodrys vernalis (Liochlorophis vernalis)

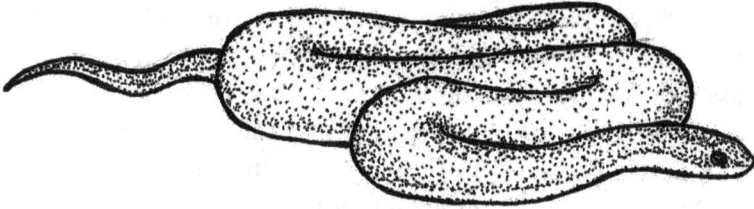

Description

This small-to-medium-size (up to 66 cm) snake is one of Prince Edward County's most elegant reptiles.

The Smooth Green Snake is easily recognized by its slender, bright green back and plain white or pale, yellow-washed belly. The Smooth Green Snake's sleek and brilliant appearance is enhanced by its immaculately smooth scales. The Smooth Green Snake prefers damp fields and meadows, often not far from water or the edges of woodlots. It frequently hunts spiders and insects while climbing in the branches of low shrubs.

On a taxonomic note, recent work by American herpetologists J.C. Oldham and H. M. Smith suggests that the Smooth Green Snake is more genetically distinct than once thought from the Rough Green Snake (*Opheodrys aestivus*), a species assumed to be its more southerly cousin (see references). As Francis Cook points out, only time will tell if the researchers' proposal to classify the Smooth Green Snake into a separate genus (*Liochlorophis*) is more generally accepted.

Distribution

The Smooth Green Snake is likely rare in Prince Edward County, but with a locally healthy population of the species in the undisturbed scrub and meadowlands at the Prince Edward Point National Wildlife Area.

The report of the Prince Edward County Reptile and Amphibian Survey describes the Smooth Green Snake as the survey team's "most elusive quarry." Despite the summer-long expectation of encountering the snake, none was found at all 190 sites surveyed until a male was collected during a late-October warm-spell at Prince Edward Point that same autumn. The report also mentions that four or five Smooth Green Snakes were spotted by naturalists working at Prince Edward Point National Wildlife Area throughout the summer. Other older records for the snake near Ameliasburgh and near Glenora in 1978 are also included in the report, which concludes that the snake is "probably not common in the County."

The Ontario Herpetofaunal Summary notes four records for the Smooth Green Snake since the Reptile and Amphibian Survey. Three of these are again from the Prince Edward Point National Wildlife Area in 1984 and 1985. Another is a report from Thomas A. Huff of the Reptile Breeding Foundation who found one near Allisonville in 1987. The Smooth Green Snake is also mentioned in the Ontario Ministry of Natural Resources' 1973 *Ecological and Geological Overview of Prince Edward County*.

Researchers with the Royal Ontario Museum's 1941 *Faunal Investigation of Prince Edward County, Ontario* did not find any Smooth Green Snakes in their search of the County. The survey's report mentions that County resident W.J. Palmer caught one at Hallowell, halfway between Picton and Bloomfield, and that local naturalist Grant Carman described seeing one in 1936 in a letter dated the following year.

The report concludes "there is no reason to doubt that it is commoner than this information would indicate."

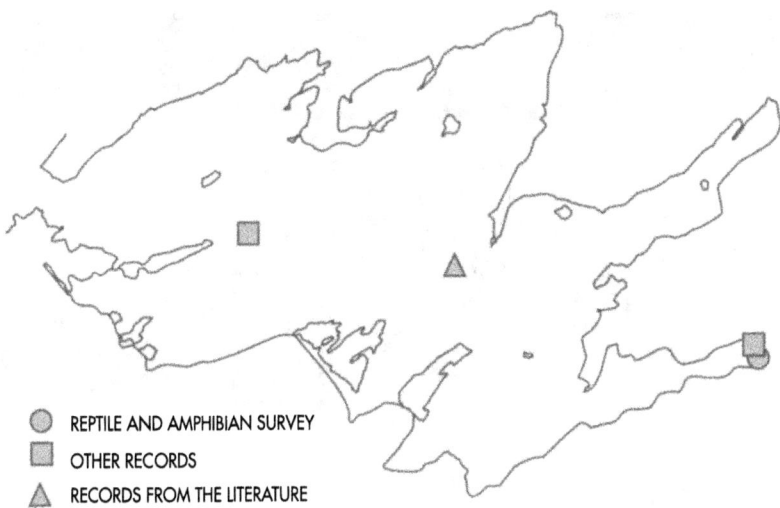

REPTILE AND AMPHIBIAN SURVEY
OTHER RECORDS
RECORDS FROM THE LITERATURE

Eastern Milk Snake
Lampropeltis triangulum triangulum

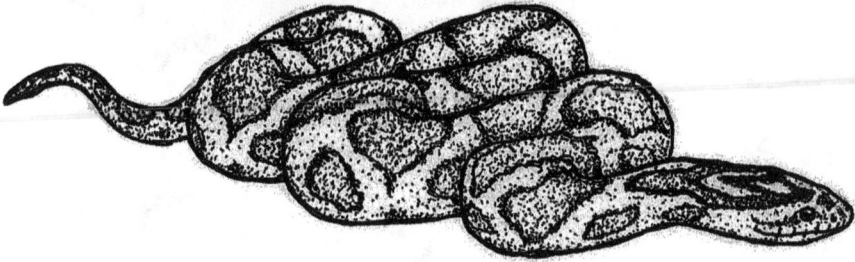

Description

This handsome, medium-sized (up to 132.1 cm) and harmless snake is best known—and much maligned—for its unnerving habit of vibrating its tail like a rattlesnake when confronted.

The Eastern Milk Snake is best recognized by its large reddish brown, black-bordered blotches on its grey-to-brown back which alternate with smaller blotches down its sides. It often has a light V or Y design toward the back of its head. The Milk Snake's belly has a distinctive checkerboard, black-on-white pattern down its length. The Eastern Milk Snake is found in meadows or around County farm buildings, where it is likely hunting barnyard mice—not milking cows, as was once believed.

Distribution

The Eastern Milk Snake is uncommon but nevertheless widespread in Prince Edward County. The Milk Snake's somewhat secretive habits tend to make encountering one a relatively infrequent occurrence.

The Prince Edward County Reptile and Amphibian Survey found only 14 individuals at 11 of 190 sites sampled. All of these records were concentrated in the southern half of the County and most were in the southeast corner. A lone Milk Snake was uncovered on Main Duck Island. The survey's report concludes that Milk Snakes "are probably more common than these results indicate" but offers no explanation for this opinion.

The Ontario Herpetofaunal Summary has compiled 16 additional records for the Eastern Milk Snake in Prince Edward County since the Reptile and Amphibian Survey. Besides one found dead on the road near Ameliasburgh and another killed on the road near Demorestville, these records are again concentrated in the southern half of the island.

The Ontario Ministry of Natural Resources uncovered the Milk Snake in its wetland survey in the Ameliasburgh area in August 1993. Other records for the Milk Snake from the literature and elsewhere are also from the northern half of Prince Edward County. The snake is reported near Consecon in the ministry's 1975 watershed survey of the Consecon Creek drainage system and mention of the species is included in the ministry's 1973 *Ecological and Geological Overview of Prince Edward County.*

The Royal Ontario Museum's 1941 *Faunal Investigation of Prince Edward County, Ontario* mentions that two Milk Snakes were collected near Lake Consecon in 1930 and another was collected at Garrett Island at West Lake in that same year. The investigation's report concludes that "the species must be commoner than these few records would suggest."

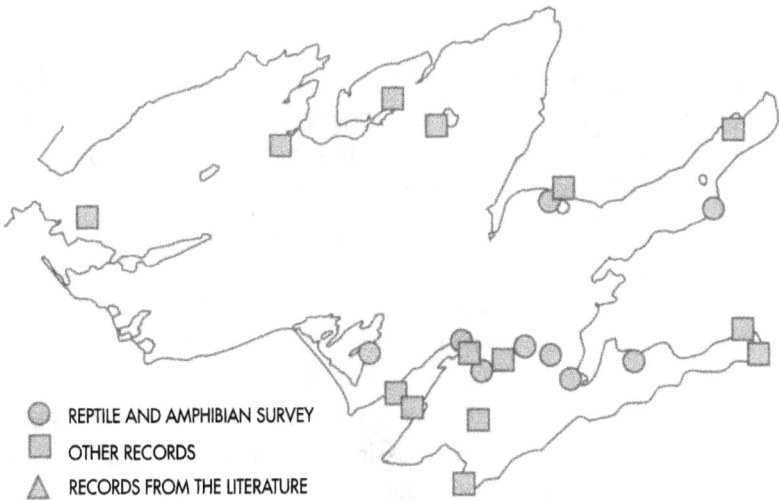

○ REPTILE AND AMPHIBIAN SURVEY
▢ OTHER RECORDS
△ RECORDS FROM THE LITERATURE

NEWTS AND SALAMANDERS
Mudpuppy
Necturus maculosus maculosus

Description

This large (up to 48.6 cm), curious-looking amphibian is Prince Edward County's only completely aquatic salamander.

The Mudpuppy is most easily recognized by its extraordinary size and by it external gills which are found only in the larval stage of other salamanders. Otherwise, its body is plain pale grey to brown with a scattering of black spots. The Mudpuppy is most frequently found in the shallows of permanent bodies of water, such as lakes, ponds and rivers.

Distribution

The Mudpuppy is uncommon but with localized healthy populations in some of the waters in and around Prince Edward County. Its secretive, nocturnal, aquatic habits no doubt contribute to limiting the likelihood of encountering one.

The Prince Edward County Reptile and Amphibian Survey found adult and larval Mudpuppies at one of 190 sites sampled and larvae only at one other. The first of these two sites, at the east end of Lake Consecon at Melville, revealed three Mudpuppies which were discovered under the large flat rocks littering the shallows of the creek outlet there. The ease with which these were found gave the impression that the outlet supported a healthy number of the animals. Mudpuppy larvae were also captured by the survey team in the waters of the Bay of Quinte just west of Glenora. And a group of fishermen provided what the survey's report calls "a reliable report" of Mudpuppies caught in East Lake. The report concludes that Mudpuppies "are almost certainly more widespread than this survey indicates."

The Ontario Herpetofaunal Summary adds one other record for the Mudpuppy in Prince Edward County since the Reptile and Amphibian Survey. This was reported by Thomas A. Huff of the Reptile Breeding Foundation who observed one of the large salamanders at the mouth of the Sawguin Creek south of Rossmore in the spring of 1987.

The Ontario Ministry of Natural Resources' watershed survey of the Big Island Marsh in August 1993 reported discovering mudpuppies there. Mention of the occurrence of the species in the area is also included in the ministry's 1973 *Ecological and Geological Overview of Prince Edward County*.

The researchers with the Royal Ontario Museum's 1941 *Faunal Investigation of Prince Edward County, Ontario* describe the Mudpuppy as "not much in evidence" in the summer of 1930 when they did their field work. They mention two Mudpuppy specimens collected in the County, one (25.5 cm) in 1930 and another captured at Hallowell (27 cm) by H.P. Stovell in 1932. The investigation's report uses observations of the animal by area residents to conclude that "the species is more abundant than this meagre collection would indicate." Among these is a letter from Homer Thomas describing a large number of Mudpuppies visible under the ice near Wellington in December 1930. Another letter written by J.F. Brimley in January 1940 says the aquatic salamander was "very plentiful in West Lake" and describes it as having been "a great annoyance" for the previous 20 to 25 winters because of its tendency to get hooked on ice fishing line.

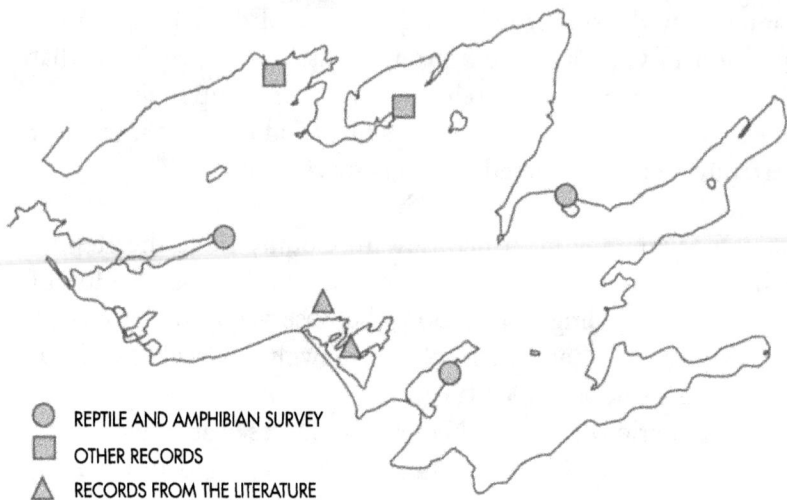

REPTILE AND AMPHIBIAN SURVEY
OTHER RECORDS
RECORDS FROM THE LITERATURE

Blue-Spotted/Jefferson Salamander
Ambystoma laterale-jeffersonianum complex

Description

The medium-sized (up to 21 cm), woodland salamander complex described here includes the Blue-Spotted Salamander (*Ambystoma laterale*) and a self-cloning female hybrid between this species and its more southerly cousin, the Jefferson Salamander (*Ambystoma jeffersonianum*).

Since the peculiar ecology of these animals is too complicated to consider in any detail here (instead see Anthony (1991) in the references) and because of the difficulty in readily and reliably distinguishing between Blue-Spotted Salamanders from hybrids in the field, they are considered together. Suffice to say that Jim Bogart, a professor at the University of Guelph who has studied this salamander complex from Prince Edward County and across the province, estimates that Blue-Spotted Salamanders make up some 85 percent of the population in this area, while triploid hybrids (that is, female hybrids with an extra set of chromosomes) account for the remaining 15 percent.

Salamanders in the Blue-Spotted/Jefferson Complex are most easily recognized by the bluish flecks or spots along the sides and tails of their black to dusky grey bodies. The Blue-Spotted/Jefferson Salamander prefers hiding under rocks and logs in damp woodlots and wooded ravines, usually not far from ponds or temporary pools and ditches where the salamander's eggs and larvae are found in the spring.

Distribution

The Blue-Spotted/Jefferson Salamander is common and widely distributed throughout Prince Edward County woodlands.

The Prince Edward County Reptile and Amphibian Survey found Blue-Spotted/Jefferson Salamanders at 27 of 190 sites sampled. None of the species were uncovered at sites in the northwest corner of the island. Many of the survey's total of 46 records were for salamander larvae collected in a variety of County ponds and wetlands and later identified in the lab. Adult salamanders were found near Highway 49 north of Picton, at MacCauley Mountain, near Cressy, at Lost Lake, at Black River, near Point Petre, at Little Bluff and at Prince Edward Point. The survey's interim report concludes that Blue-Spotted/Jefferson Salamander is "common throughout the area" with the exception of Ameliasburgh and vicinity.

The Ontario Herpetofaunal Summary has compiled 11 additional records for the Blue-Spotted/Jefferson Salamander complex in Prince Edward County since the Reptile and Amphibian Survey. The Summary also includes one confirmed record of a genetically identified Blue-Spotted Salamander found near Cherry Valley and three records confirmed for the Blue-Spotted/Jefferson triploid female hybrid (with two Blue-Spotted Salamander sets of chromosomes and one from the Jefferson Salamander).

The Blue-Spotted/Jefferson Salamander was uncovered during the Ontario Ministry of Natural Resources wetland surveys of Ameliasburgh (August 1993), the nearby Albury Swamp (July 1993), the Big Swamp (June 1984, 1986) and near Petticoat Point (August 1993). Salamanders of the Blue-Spotted/Jefferson Complex were also encountered by Fiona Burrows in her 1981 reptile and amphibian research at the Prince Edward Point National Wildlife Area. Other records for the Blue-Spotted/Jefferson Salamander are included in the Ontario Ministry of Natural Resources' 1973 *Ecological and Geological Overview of Prince Edward County* and in the ministry's 1976 survey of the Black River watershed system.

Researchers with the Royal Ontario Museum's 1941 *Faunal Investigation of Prince Edward County, Ontario* collected specimens of Blue-Spotted/Jefferson Salamander (described at the time as Jefferson Salamanders) near Hallowell and Picton and at West Lake. The report also mentions a specimen collected from Hallowell in 1932 by H.P. Stovell. The investigation concludes that the salamander "would be found to be common enough in the spawning season although it is not much in evidence later in the year."

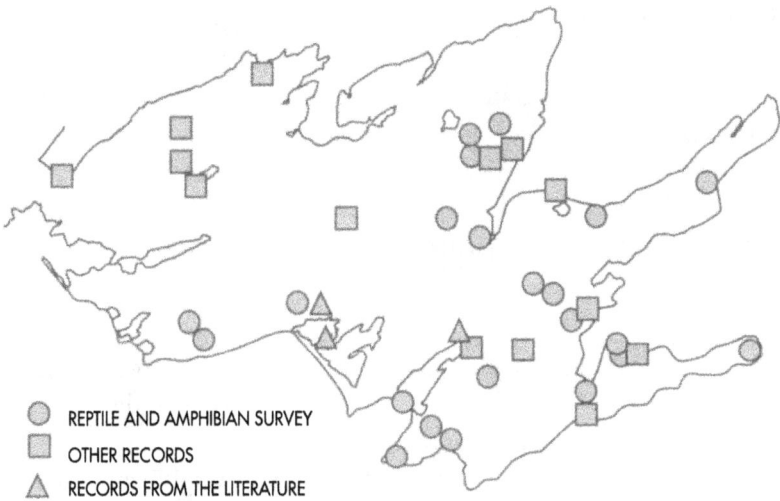

○ REPTILE AND AMPHIBIAN SURVEY
☐ OTHER RECORDS
△ RECORDS FROM THE LITERATURE

Spotted Salamander
Ambystoma maculatum

Description

This mid-sized-to-large (up to 24.8 cm), plump salamander is one of Prince Edward County's most impressive amphibians.

The Spotted Salamander, also known as the Yellow-Spotted Salamander, is best recognized by its yellow or orange spots roughly aligned in rows along either side of its black body. The Spotted Salamander is usually found under wet woodland logs and rocks, typically not far from ponds, streams or open water.

Distribution

The Spotted Salamander is rare in Prince Edward County, and the small number of records for this secretive salamander appear to be confined to southeast corner of the area.

The Prince Edward County Reptile and Amphibian Survey found single adult Spotted Salamanders at two of 190 sites sampled. The first was uncovered, along with a Blue-Spotted/Jefferson Salamander (*Ambystoma laterale-jeffersonianum* complex) under a log in a maple and beech forest near Black River on August 30, 1979. The other was found in a small wooded area on the edge of Lake-On-The-Mountain in September of that year. None of the many salamander larvae collected from area ponds were positively identified as young Spotted Salamanders. The survey's report concludes that considerable further work needs to be done to determine the distribution and status of the Spotted Salamander in the County.

The Ontario Herpetofaunal Summary adds just two other records for the Spotted Salamander in Prince Edward County since the Reptile and Amphibian Survey was conducted. Both were reported by Thomas Huff of the Reptile Breeding Foundation who observed the animals near Demorestville and near Glenora in the spring of 1987.

Area wetland surveys by the Ontario Ministry of Natural Resources between 1984 and 1993 uncovered reports of the Spotted Salamander near Black River (1993), Cressy (June 1984), and Lake-On-The-Mountain (July 1993). Mention of the Spotted Salamander as a resident salamander species is also included in the ministry's 1973 *Ecological and Geological Overview of Prince Edward County*.

Researchers with the Royal Ontario Museum's 1941 *Faunal Investigation of Prince Edward County, Ontario* encountered no Spotted Salamanders during their exploration of the area in 1930. The investigation report mentions, however, that area naturalist W.J. LeRay reported that he collected one in deep woods near Cressy in 1939.

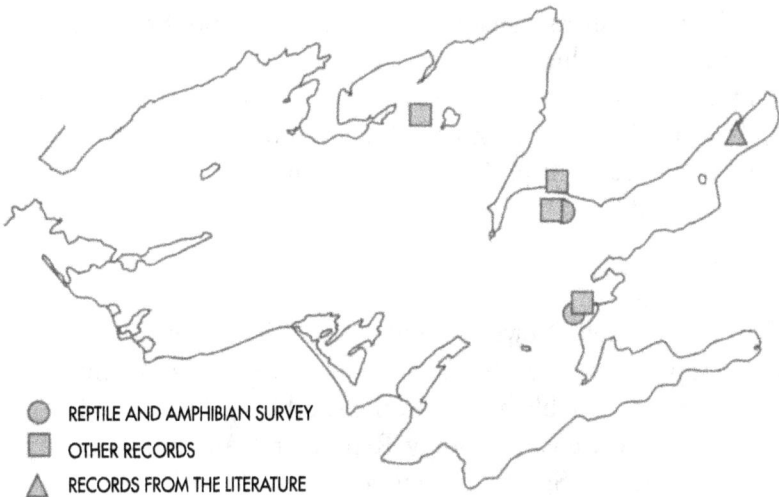

⬤ REPTILE AND AMPHIBIAN SURVEY
▢ OTHER RECORDS
△ RECORDS FROM THE LITERATURE

Red-Spotted Newt
Notophthalmus viridescens viridescens

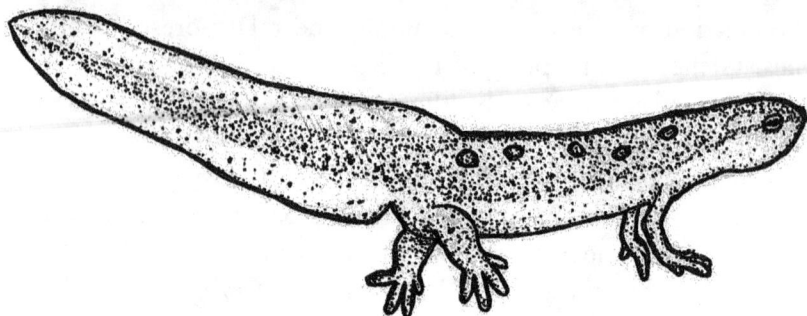

Description

This small (up to 14 cm), largely aquatic salamander is among the most intriguing of all Prince Edward County amphibians.

The Red-Spotted Newt is most easily recognized by the numerous black-bordered red spots scattered on its olive-brown to yellowish-green body. Its throat and belly are yellow, often with scattered black dots. During the land stage of this attractive salamander, the animal is known as the Red Eft and is differently coloured than its aquatic phase. The eft is bright orange to dark red with the black-bordered, red spots still visible. The Red-Spotted Newt is found in permanent or semi-permanent waters such as ponds, marshes, small lakes and slow-moving rivers and creeks. The Red Eft prefers woodlots where its lives under rotting logs and litter.

Distribution

The Red-Spotted Newt is common in Prince Edward County, but it appears to be locally abundant in many ponds, streams and other areas of suitable habitat in the southeast of the island.

The Prince Edward County Reptile and Amphibian Survey encountered Red-Spotted Newts, as adults, efts or larvae, at sites confined to the eastern side of the County, including Little Bluff,

Cressy, southeast of Fish Lake and the tributaries of Black River. Altogether, the research team reported eight records for the Newt at seven of 190 sites sampled. These were distributed mainly in the southern half of the County. The survey uncovered just one Red Eft. Nevertheless, the survey's report concludes that Red-Spotted Newts are "probably quite common" in the County.

The Ontario Herpetofaunal Summary has compiled eight other records for the Red-Spotted Newt in Prince Edward County in the years since the Reptile and Amphibian Survey. Perhaps the most remarkable record was reported by area naturalist Jon Boxall who discovered more than 50 Red Efts lying dead near freshly poured concrete at Little Bluff on October 10, 1986.

The Red-Spotted Newt was also uncovered by Fiona Burrows during her reptile and amphibian research at the Prince Edward Point National Wildlife Area in 1981. The Ontario Ministry of Natural Resources reported the Red-Spotted Newt in two of their area wetland surveys completed between 1984 and 1993. These were at Ameliasburgh and at Black River in 1993. Curiously, the Red-Spotted Newt is not included in the ministry's 1973 *Ecological and Geological Overview of Prince Edward County*.

Researchers with the Royal Ontario Museum's 1941 *Faunal Investigation of Prince Edward County, Ontario* collected Red-Spotted Newt specimens near Picton and West Lake in 1930, and local naturalist W.J. LeRay collected it at Cressy in 1939. The investigation concludes that the Red-Spotted Newt "is, no doubt, common in the County where proper ponds occur."

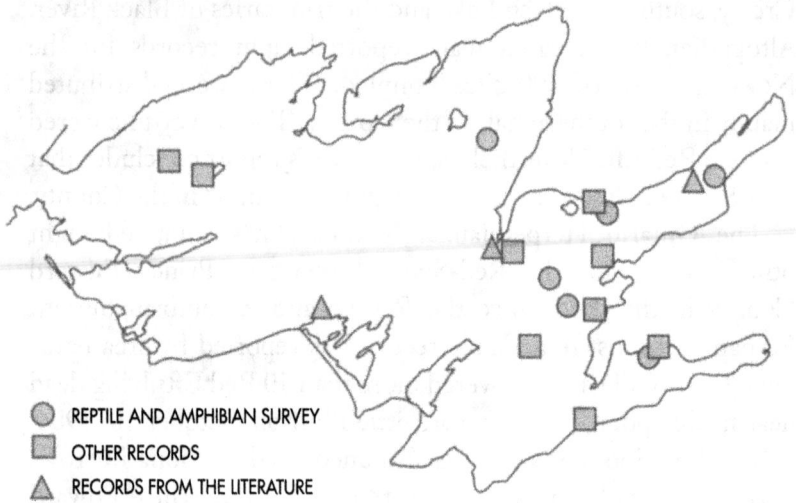

REPTILE AND AMPHIBIAN SURVEY
OTHER RECORDS
RECORDS FROM THE LITERATURE

Redback Salamander
Plethodon cinereus

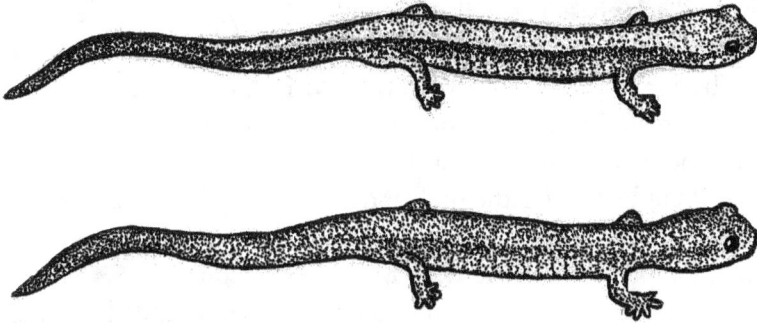

Description

This handsome, terrestrial amphibian is Prince Edward County's smallest salamander, measuring no larger than 12.7 cm.

The Redback Salamander is most often recognized by a thick, straight-edged red stripe running the length of its slender, black or dark grey back. The other colour phase of this salamander—the "Leadback" Salamander—appears uniformly dark grey to black. Unlike other County salamanders, the Redback Salamander has no aquatic larval stage and can therefore be found some distance from water. In general, the salamander prefers a variety of mature woodlots or wooded areas where it is often found hiding under rocks, logs, bark or other forest-floor litter.

Distribution

The Redback Salamander is common and widespread where suitable habitat occurs in the southeastern half of Prince Edward County.

The salamander's apparent infrequent occurrence on the western side of the island suggests the species may have a marked preference for the alkaline soil conditions of the limestone plains that characterize the south and east of the area.

The Prince Edward County Reptile and Amphibian Survey found Redback Salamanders at 14 of 190 sites sampled, none of which was much west of Picton. Both colour phases were present at the sites where the salamanders were uncovered, but the number of the redback phase generally outnumbered the number of leadback phase salamanders found at a ratio of two to one. The survey found Redback Salamanders in woodlots and ravines near Picton, near Highway 49 and North Port, at MacCauley Mountain, at Lake-On-The-Mountain, near Cressy, at Lost Lake, near Black River, near Point Petre, at Little Bluff and near Prince Edward Point. The survey's report concludes that the Redback Salamander is "very common but again in the eastern half of the County."

The Ontario Herpetofaunal Summary has compiled 17 additional records for the Redback Salamander in Prince Edward County since the Reptile and Amphibian Survey. These include a record by Michael Oldham, herpetologist with the Ontario Ministry of Natural Resources, who reported finding 82 of the salamanders with red backs, another 21 of the leadback phase and one that was an intermediate phase between the two during a visit to an Ameliasburgh-area woodlot on September 9, 1987. Another report of note is of 13 leadback phase salamanders and just one redback phase discovered by area naturalist Jon Boxall at Beaver Meadow on May 5, 1990. The report suggests the possibility that there is a predominantly leadback phase population of these salamanders in this area.

The Ontario Ministry of Natural Resources' survey of area wetlands discovered Redback Salamanders at Ameliasburgh, the nearby Albury Swamp, near Black River and near Petticoat Point. The species was also found by Fiona Burrows in her 1981 reptile and amphibian research at the Prince Edward Point National Wildlife Area. Mention of the Redback Salamander is also included in the ministry's 1973 *Ecological and Geological Overview of Prince Edward County* and in the ministry's 1988 wetlands study summary.

Researchers with the Royal Ontario Museum's 1941 *Faunal Investigation of Prince Edward County, Ontario* collected 27 specimens of the Redback Salamander near Hallowell and Wellington in 1930. Of these, 16 were collected on Garrett Island on May 23, 1930 of which six were of the leadback phase. The investigation's report also mentions that the Redback Salamander was observed between Glenora and Cressy in 1939 by area naturalist W.J. LeRay, who "reported it to be not common."

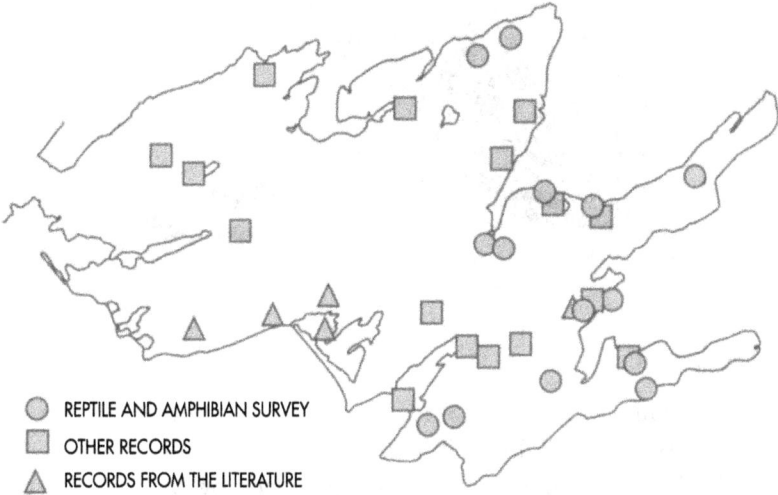

○ REPTILE AND AMPHIBIAN SURVEY
□ OTHER RECORDS
△ RECORDS FROM THE LITERATURE

TOADS AND FROGS
Eastern American Toad
Bufo americanus americanus

Description

This medium-sized (up to 11.1 cm) toad is among the most comic looking amphibians in Prince Edward County.

The Eastern American Toad is recognized by the one or two large warts in each of the largest dark spots covering its back. The toad's colouration is light to dark brown but can vary with changes in temperature and physical environment. Also distinctive are the large, raised glands behind each eye. The American Toad's song is a long, high trill which can be heard from April to June. During spring breeding, the American Toad is found in shallow bodies of water such as ditches and streams. It is, however, a mainly terrestrial amphibian and is often found some distance from water.

Distribution

The Eastern American Toad is common and widespread across Prince Edward County, although evidence from the literature suggests that it may have been considerably less so in the past.

The Prince Edward County Reptile and Amphibian Survey reported 60 records of the Eastern American Toad at 38 of 190 sites sampled in the County. These sites were evenly distributed across the island with toad tadpoles as much in evidence as adults. The survey's report concludes that the American Toad is "abundant throughout the County."

The Ontario Herpetofaunal Summary has compiled 27 additional records for the American Toad in Prince Edward County since the Reptile and Amphibian Survey, as well as five records from the early 1970s. Like the survey records, these reports appear evenly distributed across the County.

Volunteers with the Long Point Bird Observatory's Marsh Monitoring Program reported the American Toad at the Big Island Marsh in 1995 and at the Beaver Meadow in 1996. Fiona Burrows also reported repeatedly finding the American Toad during her 1981 reptile and amphibian research at the Prince Edward Point National Wildlife Area. The Ontario Ministry of Natural Resources' series of wetland evaluations between 1984 and 1993 found toads during eight of the 21 surveys that included species lists. Mention of the American Toad is also included in the Ontario Ministry of Natural Resources' 1973 *Ecological and Geological Overview of Prince Edward County* and in the ministry's 1976 Black River watershed survey.

Researchers with the Royal Ontario Museum's 1941 *Faunal Investigation of Prince Edward County, Ontario* reported "toads were scarce at all localities visited and only seven specimens were seen" during their field work in early summer 1930. These specimens were collected from Hallowell, Picton, the Sandbanks and the Bay of Quinte. Tadpoles were collected at Hallowell on May 24 and at the Sandbanks on June 25. Area naturalist W.J. LeRay told the investigators that the Toad could be seen at Cressy in 1938 and 1939 but that it was "not common there."

Toads in the County have been heard singing as early as April 12, 1988 as noted by area resident W.J. Christie near Cressy. Mr. Christie also reports that the earliest he heard a full chorus of Toads (breeding) was on May 5, 1988. The latest record for (breeding) Toads singing was two individuals heard on May 29, 1995 at Big Island Marsh by volunteers with the Long Point Bird Observatory's Marsh Monitoring Program. The report of the 1941 faunal survey notes that Toads "were occasionally heard" from May 23 to June 26, 1930. It also mentions that resident J.L. Baillie heard them at Milford as late as June 30, 1930.

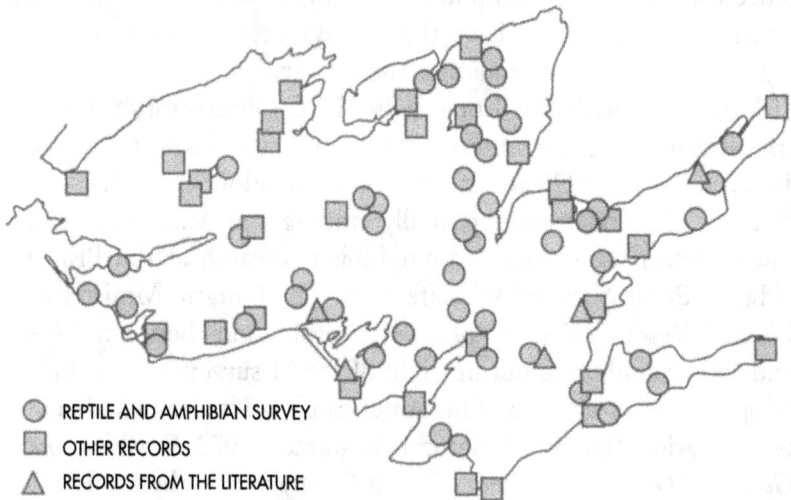

○ REPTILE AND AMPHIBIAN SURVEY
☐ OTHER RECORDS
△ RECORDS FROM THE LITERATURE

Grey Treefrog
Hyla versicolor

Description

This largest (up to 6 cm) of Prince Edward County treefrogs is the only amphibian in the area with the ability to significantly alter its colour.

The Grey Treefrog is usually grey but can vary to brilliant green, depending on its activity and physical environment. It has a distinctive white spot below its eyes and darker markings on its bump-covered back. Its call is a loud, ascending trill that can be heard from May throughout the summer and more occasionally into the autumn.

During the breeding season, the Grey Treefrog is often found in wetlands where there are small shrubs near or in shallow water for it on which it may climb. Otherwise, these frogs can be found dispersed throughout woodlots and other forested areas.

Distribution

The Grey Treefrog is common in Prince Edward County, but it is less evident outside of a number of localized areas. Its secretive, arboreal nature contributes to its low profile.

The Prince Edward County Reptile and Amphibian Survey compiled 32 records of the Grey Treefrog at 13 of the 190 sites sampled in the County. Only one adult frog was found. The other records represent tadpole observations or those of small, newly emerged frogs. The survey's report concludes that the Grey Treefrog is "fairly widespread in the County."

The Ontario Herpetofaunal Summary has compiled 25 additional records for the Grey Treefrog in Prince Edward County since the Reptile and Amphibian Survey, as well as one record from 1972. Like the Reptile and Amphibian Survey records, these reports appear to be distributed throughout the County with the exception of the northwest corner. Volunteers with the Long Point Bird Observatory's Marsh Monitoring Program reported the Grey Treefrog at the Big Island Marsh and near Morrison Point in 1995 and in the north marsh of Big Island, Sawguin Creek and Beaver Meadow in 1996.

The Ontario Ministry of Natural Resources' series of wetland evaluations conducted in the area between 1984 and 1993 found the Grey Treefrog at seven of the 21 surveys that included species lists. Reference to the species is also included in the ministry's 1973 *Ecological and Geological Overview of Prince Edward County* and its 1976 survey of the Black River watershed system.

Researchers with the Royal Ontario Museum's 1941 *Faunal Investigation of Prince Edward County, Ontario* reported that "neither adults nor tadpoles were found" during their search for Grey Treefrogs in the area in 1930. They succeeded only in hearing the frog on four occasions. The report also mentions that area naturalist W.J. LeRay collected specimens of the Grey Treefrog at Cressy in 1939.

W.J. Christie's natural history diaries note that the Grey Treefrog has been heard calling near his Cressy-area home as early as April 19, 1976. The latest reported record for Grey Treefrogs calling in any number from W.J. Christie's pond (breeding) June 28, 1988. Visiting biologist Gavin Christie heard a lone frog calling in the forest (non-breeding "fall call") at W.J. Christie's home on a mild October 17, 1987. Researchers with the 1941

Royal Ontario Museum survey reported hearing the frog calling from marshes (breeding) on June 5, 11 and 12 at Hallowell and on June 30 near Prince Edward Point in 1930.

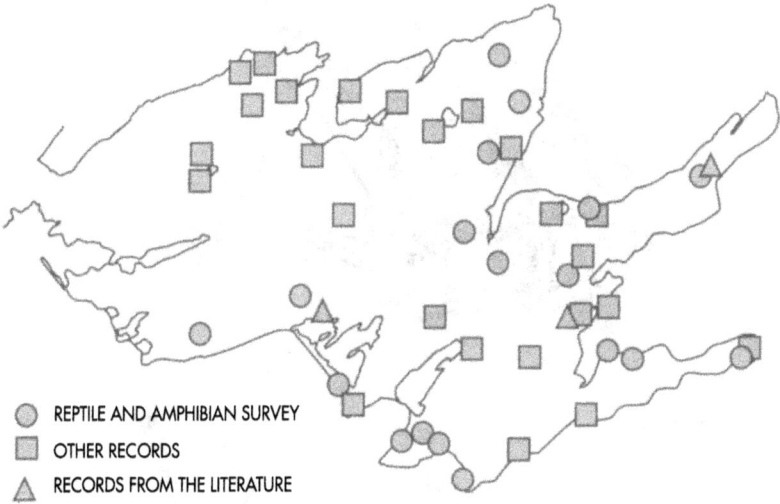

○ REPTILE AND AMPHIBIAN SURVEY
□ OTHER RECORDS
△ RECORDS FROM THE LITERATURE

Northern Spring Peeper
Pseudacris crucifer crucifer

Description

This small (up to 3.7 cm), delicate frog is nevertheless responsible for one of the boldest and most familiar sounds of springtime in Prince Edward County.

The Northern Spring Peeper is best recognized by its fragile-looking size, its padded toes and the dark, X-shaped mark on its light brown back. Its call is a high "peep...peep...peep" and can be heard in full chorus in April and May and more occasionally through to the fall. The Spring Peeper is frequently found in temporary ponds and pools during its breeding season but disperses into woodland vegetation for the remainder of the season.

Distribution

The Northern Spring Peeper is common and widespread in Prince Edward County, but its secretive habits make it difficult to find after the early spring breeding season. Historic records suggest the frog may have been less common in the past.

The Prince Edward County Reptile and Amphibian Survey compiled 17 records of the Northern Spring Peeper at 10 of 190 sites sampled in the County. These were uncovered mainly in the south and west of the area, including the Sandbanks, near Prince Edward Point, Little Bluff, Cressy and near Fish Lake. The survey's report concludes that the Spring Peeper's "distribution is probably more widespread and spring would be an ideal time to learn more."

The Ontario Herpetofaunal Summary has compiled 26 additional records for the Spring Peeper in Prince Edward County since the Reptile and Amphibian Survey, as well as five records from the early 1970s. These reports are widely distributed throughout the County. Volunteers with the Long Point Bird Observatory's Marsh Monitoring Program, meanwhile, reported hearing Spring Peepers at the Big Island Marsh and near Morrison Point in 1995.

Reference to the species is also included in the Ontario Ministry of Natural Resources' wetland evaluations of the swamp at Ameliasburgh (August 1993), Black River (1993) and near Petticoat Point (August 1993). It is also mentioned in the list of indigenous frog species included in the ministry's 1973 *Ecological and Geological Overview of Prince Edward County* and its 1976 survey of the Black River watershed system.

Researchers with the Royal Ontario Museum's 1941 *Faunal Investigation of Prince Edward County, Ontario* reported that the Spring Peeper "did not appear to be a plentiful element in the fauna of Prince Edward County during our visit there in 1930." The group collected tadpoles on Garrett Island in West Lake, near Picton and at the Sandbanks. The report also mentions that area naturalist W.J. LeRay told the investigators that he found the Spring Peeper at Cressy, but that it was "not common."

The Northern Spring Peeper has been heard calling (breeding) in Prince Edward County as early as April 1, 1988, when visiting biologist Gavin Christie noted a small number calling from the pond beside W.J. Christie's Cressy-area home. Singing for the frog was reported to be at its peak on April 30 of that same year in the same location, and naturalist Jim Mountjoy heard several calling from a pond (breeding) at Prince Edward Point as late as May 30, 1984. The latest record for a Spring Peeper calling (non-breeding "fall call") was noted by Michael J. Oldham of the Ontario Herpetofaunal Summary who heard a single frog calling weakly near Ameliasburgh on September 5, 1987. Researchers with the 1941 Royal Ontario Museum faunal survey of Prince Edward County reported hearing the frog singing on May 20, 21, June 3 and 11 at West Lake in 1930.

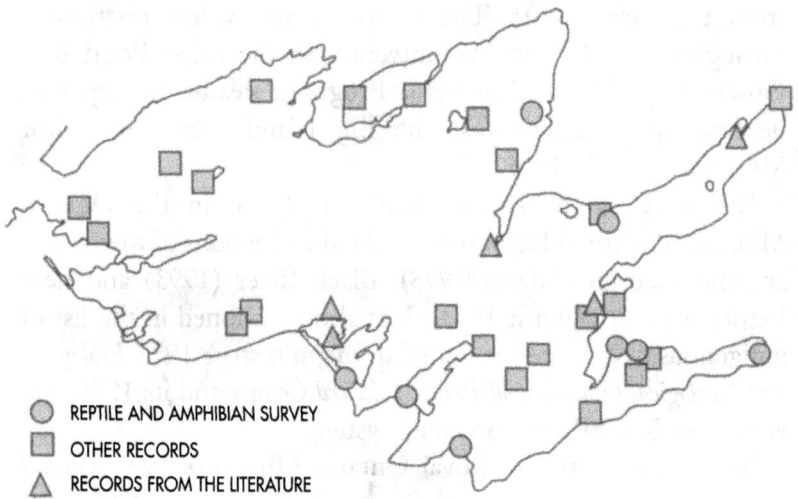

REPTILE AND AMPHIBIAN SURVEY
OTHER RECORDS
RECORDS FROM THE LITERATURE

Western Chorus Frog
Pseudacris triseriata triseriata

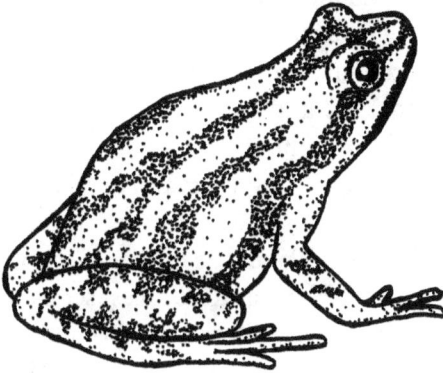

Description

The song of this small (up to 3.9 cm) frog is a dependable harbinger of springtime in Prince Edward County.

The Western Chorus Frog is normally recognized by its small size and the three dark stripes running down it's grey to dark brown back. Its surprisingly loud and rolling "prreep" call is often the first frog song of spring and can be heard from early April to late May. The Western Chorus Frog is found in shallow, often temporary bodies of water, including ponds, marshes and wet ditches during their breeding season. Otherwise, they are often found under woodland rocks and logs.

Distribution

Western Chorus Frogs are common and widespread in Prince Edward County, but they are particularly elusive after the early spring breeding season has ended.

The Prince Edward County Reptile and Amphibian Survey compiled 36 records of the Western Chorus Frog at 24 of 190 sites sampled in the County. Adults of the species were found at just one site at South Bay. Other records were for tadpoles found at a number of temporary ponds and pools widely distributed but absent from the northwest corner of the area.

The Ontario Herpetofaunal Summary has compiled 23 additional records for the Western Chorus Frog in Prince Edward County since the Reptile and Amphibian Survey, as well as five records from 1971 and 1972 and two from 1978. These reports appear to be distributed throughout the County. Meanwhile, volunteers with the Long Point Bird Observatory's Marsh Monitoring Program reported the Chorus Frog at the Big Island Marsh and near Morrison Point in 1995 and at Beaver Meadow in 1996.

The Ontario Ministry of Natural Resources' series of wetland evaluations completed for the area between 1984 and 1993 found Western Chorus Frogs at Ameliasburgh (August 1993), Black River (1993), and near Petticoat Point (August 1993). Reference to the species is also included in the ministry's 1973 *Ecological and Geological Overview of Prince Edward County*.

Researchers with the Royal Ontario Museum's 1941 *Faunal Investigation of Prince Edward County, Ontario* reported that the Western Chorus Frog "was not greatly in evidence at Prince Edward County when we arrived there on May 20, as the spawning season was then over." The group collected tadpoles and emerging frogs near Hallowell, the only locality record from the time. The report notes that area naturalist W.J. LeRay found the frog at Cressy in 1938.

The Western Chorus Frog has been heard calling in Prince Edward County as early as March 15, 1990 when area naturalist Jon Boxall noted two calling from a meadow near his home on Highway 49. W.J. Christie's natural history diaries note that the earliest date for a full chorus of the frog was April 9, 1993 at the Keller's Creek pond near his Cressy-area home. Naturalist Jim Mountjoy noted several calling from a pond (breeding) at the Prince Edward Point National Wildlife Area as late as May 30, 1984. The latest reported record for a Chorus Frog calling was noted by local resident Jon Boxall who heard a lone frog calling (non-breeding "fall call") near his home not far from Roblin Mills on October 29, 1989. Researchers with the 1941 Royal Ontario Museum survey reported hearing the frog calling sporadically from May 20 through to June 26, 1930 at Hallowell.

○ REPTILE AND AMPHIBIAN SURVEY
☐ OTHER RECORDS
△ RECORDS FROM THE LITERATURE

Bullfrog
Rana catesbeiana

Description

This impressive amphibian is the largest frog in Prince Edward County, measuring up to 20.3 cm long.

The Bullfrog's large size is often its most distinctive characteristic. It is also recognized by its uniform green back and a fold which extends from the rear of the eye down over the eardrum. Unlike the Green Frog (*Rana clamitans melanota*), the Bullfrog does not have a ridge running down either side of its back. Its call is a deep "chug-a-rug" that can be heard from mid-May through to the end of July. Bullfrogs prefer larger bodies of water and can be found along the reedy shorelines of bays, lakes and ponds.

Distribution

The Bullfrog can be considered common and widely distributed in Prince Edward County, but it is far less abundant than many other frogs in the area. Many years of exploitation by fisherman who eat or sell the frog's legs may have hurt the local population (see below).

The Prince Edward County Reptile and Amphibian Survey compiled 43 records of the Bullfrog at 35 of 190 sites sampled in the County. These were from areas of suitable habitat across much of the island. Bullfrog observations were notably absent from the central western portion of the County, an area that roughly coincides with the sand plain stretching west of Picton. The survey's report concludes that the Bullfrog "is found in many areas in the County, although nowhere did we find anything like large numbers of them."

The Ontario Herpetofaunal Summary has compiled 19 additional records for the Bullfrog in Prince Edward County since the Reptile and Amphibian Survey, as well as three from the early 1970s. These reports appear to be distributed throughout the County. Volunteers with the Long Point Bird Observatory's Marsh Monitoring Program reported the Bullfrog at the Big Island Marsh in 1995 and at the north marsh of Big Island, Sawguin Creek and Beaver Meadow in 1996.

The Bullfrog is repeatedly mentioned in the Ontario Ministry of Natural Resources' series of wetland evaluations completed for the area between 1984 and 1993. Of the 21 surveys that include species lists, 13 uncovered evidence of Bullfrogs in County marshes and swamps. Reference to the species is also included in the ministry's 1973 *Ecological and Geological Overview of Prince Edward County* and its 1976 Black River watershed evaluation.

The Royal Ontario Museum's 1941 *Faunal Investigation of Prince Edward County, Ontario* reported collecting two adult Bullfrogs and three tadpoles of the species in 1930. These were taken at a marsh somewhere in Hallowell and another location on the Bay of Quinte. The report mentions collecting specimens at a stream five kilometres west of Wellington, at a creek south of Picton and at Pleasant Bay. It also notes that area naturalist W.J. LeRay told the investigators that the Bullfrog could be seen at Cressy in 1938 and 1939, but that it was "not common."

W.J. Christie's natural history diaries note the earliest record of a Bullfrog calling as May 12, 1979 at his Cressy-area home. The Marsh Monitoring Program also reported two Bullfrogs calling on May 12, 1996. The latest reported record for Bullfrog calls was noted by researchers with the Prince Edward County Reptile and Amphibian

Survey at Black River on August 10, 1979. In 1930, researchers with the Royal Ontario Museum survey of Prince Edward County reported hearing the frog on June 3, 5, 11, 12, 13 and 14 in 1930.

Before a provincial ban on commercial fishing for Bullfrogs was imposed in 1995 and fishing the frogs for personal use was outlawed in 1996, populations of this species were in notable decline in many areas of Ontario. Data provided by Todd Norris, an ecologist with the Ministry of Natural Resources in Kingston who was instrumental in ending the harvest, shows Prince Edward County and the surrounding area may not have been as hard hit by fishermen as other regions (particularly in southwestern and southeastern Ontario) where in some cases the species was effectively extirpated. Nevertheless, between 4,000 and 20,000 frogs were taken in this district every year from 1977 (when records were kept) to 1994 (before the ban was imposed). While the harvest numbers give an equivocal account of a changing Bullfrog population (shifts in area boundaries and in fishing intensity confuse the data), it is clear the slow-to-mature Bullfrog has been under considerable pressure here. With the ban now in place and with some luck, observers may yet see an improvement in the numbers of this impressive frog within the next few years.

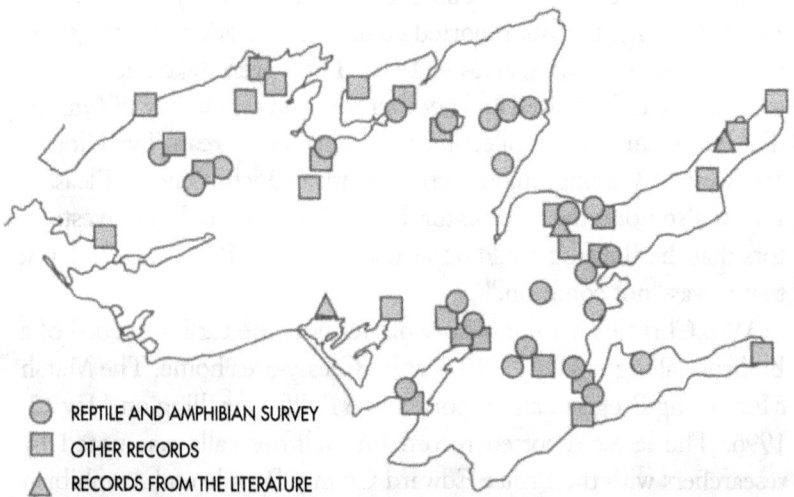

○ REPTILE AND AMPHIBIAN SURVEY
☐ OTHER RECORDS
△ RECORDS FROM THE LITERATURE

Description

This medium-sized (up to 10.8 cm) frog is a regular sight along the grassy shores of Prince Edward County ponds and marshes.

The Green Frog is best recognized by its uniformly greenish-brown back, usually with black spots scattered on it and along its sides. A ridge running along either side of the back distinguishes this frog from the Bullfrog (*Rana catesbeiana*). Its call is an explosive twang or gulp that can be heard from mid-May through to July. Green Frogs prefer shallow, marshy water such as weedy ponds and swamps and along the edges of lakes and rivers.

Distribution

The Green Frog is common and widespread in Prince Edward County, appearing in most areas of suitable habitat throughout the area.

The Prince Edward County Reptile and Amphibian Survey reported 75 records of the Green Frog at 34 of 190 sites sampled in the County. These represented almost all areas of suitable habitat distributed across the County and visited during the survey. The survey's report concludes that the Green Frog is "widely distributed and very common."

The Ontario Herpetofaunal Summary has compiled 14 additional records for the Green Frog in Prince Edward County since the Reptile and Amphibian Survey, as well as two from the early 1970s. Like the survey records, these reports appear to be distributed throughout the County. Volunteers with the Long Point Bird Observatory's Marsh Monitoring Program reported the Green Frog at the Big Island Marsh and near Morrison Point in 1995 and at the north marsh of Big Island, Sawguin Creek and Beaver Meadow in 1996. Fiona Burrows also reported repeatedly finding the Green Frog during her 1981 reptile and amphibian research at the Prince Edward Point National Wildlife Area.

The Ontario Ministry of Natural Resources' series of wetland evaluations carried out between 1984 and 1993 found evidence of the Green Frog at 11 of the 21 surveys that included species lists. These were of marshes and swamps well distributed across the County. The species is also mentioned in the ministry's 1973 *Ecological and Geological Overview of Prince Edward County* and its 1976 survey of the Black River watershed.

Researchers with the Royal Ontario Museum's 1941 *Faunal Investigation of Prince Edward County, Ontario* reported that "the Green Frog was plentiful at West Lake marsh but was not noted to be so at other places visited in 1930." The report mentions collecting specimens at a stream five kilometres west of Wellington, at a creek south of Picton and at Pleasant Bay. H.J. Dignan is mentioned collecting four specimens from somewhere in Prince Edward County in 1928. The report also notes that area naturalist W.J. LeRay told the investigators that the Green Frog could be seen at Cressy in 1938 and 1939, but that it was "not common."

Green Frogs in the County have been heard singing as early as May 5, 1993 near Cressy as reported in W.J. Christie's natural history diaries. The latest record for calls was reported by the Prince Edward County Reptile and Amphibian Survey at Black

River on August 2, 1979. The 1941 faunal investigation of Prince Edward County reported hearing the frog on June 3, 5, 11, 12, 13 and 14 in 1930.

Despite the apparently healthy numbers of Green Frogs in Prince Edward County today, there may yet be some causes for concern. The Reptile and Amphibian Survey of 1979 repeatedly discovered Green Frogs in isolated populations that appeared to lack irises or suffered from other eye anomalies and deformities, suggesting the adverse effects of toxic pollution. As with other amphibians, habitat loss appears to be another growing threat, while an unknown—but invariably large—quantity of these frogs are legally harvested and sold for fish bait every year. The impact of these factors needs thorough review to ensure these animals are not already signalling the approach of more serious trouble in their numbers.

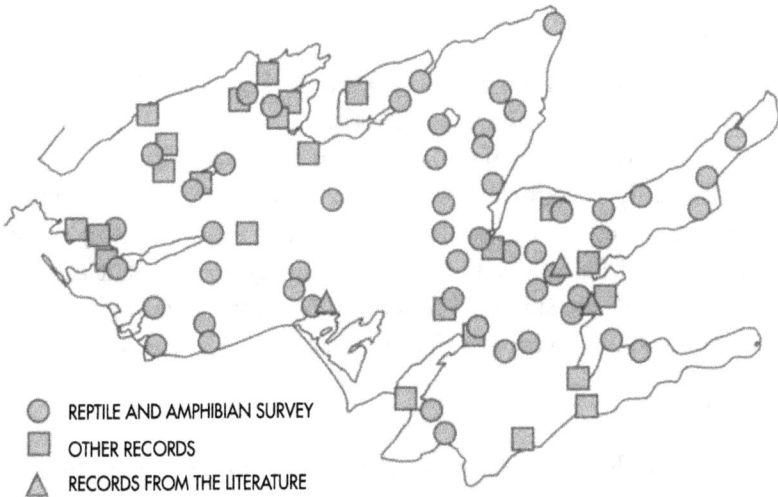

○ REPTILE AND AMPHIBIAN SURVEY
▢ OTHER RECORDS
△ RECORDS FROM THE LITERATURE

Wood Frog
Rana sylvatica

Description

This medium-sized (up to 8.3 cm), masked frog is a shy resident of Prince Edward County woodlands.

The Wood Frog is tan to dark brown over most of its body and is most easily recognized by the black bandit's mask extending back from its eye to its shoulder. It also has a ridge running along either side of its tan back. Its call is a hoarse quack that can be heard through the spring. The Wood Frog can be found in damp County woodlots with wet depressions or slow streams.

Distribution

The Wood Frog is common and fairly widespread in Prince Edward County, although its secretive habits may make this fact less apparent.

The Prince Edward County Reptile and Amphibian Survey reported 31 records of the Wood Frog at 22 of 190 sites sampled in the County. These sites were quite evenly distributed across the island with adults found at Big Swamp, near Highway 49, near Picton, near Melville, at Cressy and near Point Petre. The survey's report concludes that the Wood Frog is "quite common in the County," an opinion based principally on the wide distribution of tadpoles.

The Ontario Herpetofaunal Summary has compiled nine additional records for the Wood Frog in Prince Edward County since the Reptile and Amphibian Survey, as well as one from the early 1970s. Like the survey records, these reports appear to come from all over the County. Volunteers with the Long Point Bird Observatory's Marsh Monitoring Program reported hearing the Wood Frog at Grenade Point in 1995.

The Ontario Ministry of Natural Resources' series of wetland evaluations carried out in the County between 1984 and 1993 found evidence of Wood Frogs at Albury Swamp (July 1993), Black River (1993), Lake-On-The-Mountain (July 1993), near Petticoat Point (August 1993), near Muscote Bay (August 1992) and at Wellers Bay (August 1993). Mention of the Wood Frog is also included in ministry's list of indigenous frogs included in its 1973 *Ecological and Geological Overview of Prince Edward County*.

Researchers with the Royal Ontario Museum's 1941 *Faunal Investigation of Prince Edward County, Ontario* collected 20 adult Wood Frog specimens from the vicinities of Hallowell, Wellington, Pleasant Bay and Picton in 1930. They also collected tadpoles from a woodland pond near Wellington. Area naturalist W.J. LeRay told the investigators that he found the Wood Frog at Cressy in 1938 and 1939, but that it was "uncommon there."

A full chorus of Wood Frogs has been reported calling in the County as early as March 30 near Morrison Point (in 1995 by volunteers with the Long Point Bird Observatory Marsh Monitoring Program). Peter Christie noted that a few individuals of the species were heard quacking their hoarse call near Keller's Creek in Cressy as late as mid May 1987. This frog is also known to call occasionally (non-breeding "fall calls") on warm, wet days in the autumn.

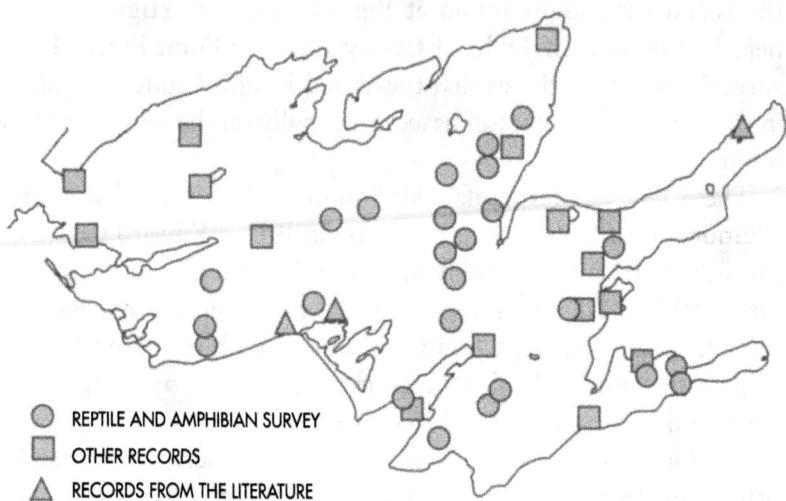

○ REPTILE AND AMPHIBIAN SURVEY
□ OTHER RECORDS
△ RECORDS FROM THE LITERATURE

Northern Leopard Frog
Rana pipiens

Description

This ubiquitous, medium-sized (up to 11.1 cm) frog is Prince Edward County's most frequently encountered amphibian.

The Northern Leopard Frog is most easily recognized by the dark spots outlined in yellow covering its brown or green back. It also has two light-coloured ridges running along either side of the back. Its call is best described as a rattling snore and can be heard from April through to early summer. The Northern Leopard Frog is found almost anywhere there is sufficient water, including ponds, marshes, streams, lakes and wet meadows.

Distribution

The Northern Leopard Frog is common and widespread throughout Prince Edward County.

The Prince Edward County Reptile and Amphibian Survey compiled 177 records of the Leopard Frog at 107 of 190 sites sampled in the County. More than any other species, the

Leopard Frog was a reliable presence most any place of suitable habitat visited by the researchers. The survey's report concludes that the Northern Leopard Frog is "undoubtedly the most numerically abundant amphibian in the County." It also notes that foot deformities, including missing toes or stump feet, were found to affect "a small percentage of the population" throughout the area, suggesting the widespread affects of toxic pollution.

The Ontario Herpetofaunal Summary has compiled 48 additional records for the Northern Leopard Frog in Prince Edward County since the Reptile and Amphibian Survey, as well as 19 records noted earlier. Like those of the Reptile and Amphibian Survey, these reports appear to be distributed throughout the County. Volunteers with the Long Point Bird Observatory's Marsh Monitoring Program reported the Northern Leopard Frog at the Big Island Marsh and near Morrison Point in 1995 and at the north marsh of Big Island, Sawguin Creek and Beaver Meadow in 1996. The frog was also found throughout the summer during the 1981 reptile and amphibian research at the Prince Edward Point National Wildlife Area.

The Ontario Ministry of Natural Resources' series of wetland evaluations completed in the area between 1984 and 1993 confirmed that the population of Northern Leopard Frogs is widespread. Of the 21 surveys that include species lists, 16 mention the presence of Leopard Frogs in County marshes and swamps. Reference to the species is also included in the Ontario Ministry of Natural Resources' 1973 *Ecological and Geological Overview of Prince Edward County* and its 1976 Black River watershed evaluation.

The Royal Ontario Museum's 1941 *Faunal Investigation of Prince Edward County, Ontario* reported collecting 23 adult Leopard Frogs near Hallowell, Wellington, Pleasant Bay, Consecon and the Sandbanks in the summer of 1930. It was also seen at other locations. The report notes that the Leopard Frog "was by far the commonest amphibian in the County, frequenting the usual variety of situations in which it might be expected." It also mentions that area naturalist W.J. LeRay told the investigators that the Leopard Frog could be seen at Cressy, but that it was "not plentiful."

The Northern Leopard Frog has been heard calling in Prince Edward County as early as March 21, 1987, when Gavin Christie noted a number calling from roadside ditches near Cherry Valley. W.J. Christie's natural history diaries note the earliest full chorus on April 15, 1976 at his Cressy-area home. The latest reported record for Leopard Frog calls was noted by researchers with the Prince Edward County Reptile and Amphibian Survey near Bloomfield on July 25, 1979.

Despite the apparently healthy numbers of Leopard Frogs in Prince Edward County today, there may yet be some causes for concern. The Reptile and Amphibian Survey of 1979 repeatedly discovered isolated populations of Northern Leopard Frogs that suffered from foot and leg deformities suggesting the adverse effects of toxic pollution. As with other amphibians, habitat loss appears to be another growing threat, while an unknown—but invariably large—quantity of these frogs are legally harvested and sold for fish bait every year. The impact of these factors needs thorough review to ensure these animals are not already signalling the approach of more serious trouble in their numbers.

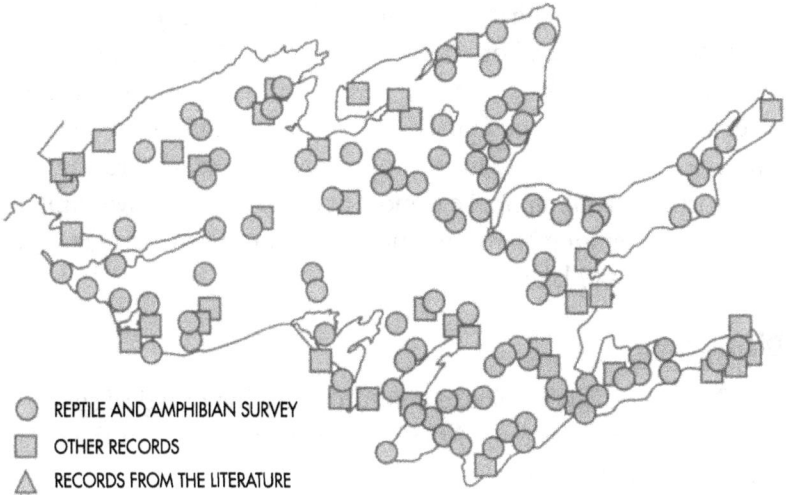

○ REPTILE AND AMPHIBIAN SURVEY
☐ OTHER RECORDS
△ RECORDS FROM THE LITERATURE

Northern Ribbon Snake
Thamnophis sauritus septentrionalis

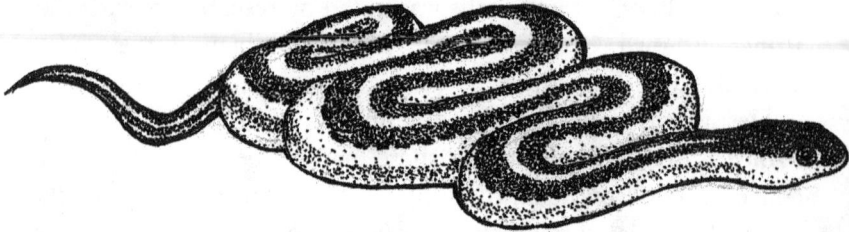

Description

This medium-sized (up to about 95 cm), semi-aquatic snake is known for its skittish nature and quickness.

At first glance, the Northern Ribbon Snake may look very like the Eastern Garter Snake (*Thamnophis sirtalis sirtalis*) with a yellow stripe running down its black back and another on each side. But the Ribbon Snake is most easily distinguished from its much more common cousin by its slenderness, its significantly longer tail (up to a third of the snake's body length) and by side stripes running along the third and fourth row of scales (counting up from the belly) instead of along rows two and three as they do in the Garter Snake. The Northern Ribbon Snake also has much paler lip scales than the Garter Snake and has a crescent-shaped white mark immediately in front of its eye. If encountered at all, the Northern Ribbon Snake is most likely to be found swimming or slithering among the shoreline reeds and grasses of marshes, ponds, rivers and lakes.

Distribution

The Northern Ribbon Snake is considered a hypothetical species for Prince Edward County; that is, encountering one in the area is exceptionally unlikely.

Although the County is well within the range of this sly snake, there is only one record of the Northern Ribbon Snake for the area. All other past and recent attempts to uncover another, including the travels of the researchers with the Prince Edward County Reptile and Amphibian Survey, have been unsuccessful. The first and only Ribbon Snake found in Prince Edward County was collected by D.C. Benedetti near the mouth of Sawguin Creek, south of Rossmore on October 14, 1979. The specimen was sent to the reptile collection of the University of Guelph. Unfortunately, recent attempts to locate this specimen (collection catalogue number UG647) in order to confirm its identity have been unsuccessful.

While the fact that a specimen was taken and the fact that the habitat in which the snake was found (that is, at Sawguin Creek) both add to the veracity of the record, there may be reasons to doubt it. The most obvious of these is the snake's superficial resemblance to the Eastern Garter Snake (*Thamnophis sirtalis sirtalis*). A particularly slender member of that much more common snake might easily be mistaken for a Ribbon Snake by a collector unfamiliar with the species. The second reason for scepticism concerning this record is the unlikely coincidence that the same collector captured the County's only known specimen of Pickerel Frog (*Rana palustris*), which was also sent to the University of Guelph and also unaccounted for. Finally, it remains curious that no other Ribbon Snakes have turned up in the area, which has since become a more regular destination for interested naturalists.

There is no mention of the Northern Ribbon Snake in the Ontario Ministry of Natural Resources' 1973 *Ecological and Geological Overview of Prince Edward County*. Similarly, the Royal Ontario Museum's 1941 *Faunal Investigation of Prince Edward County, Ontario* does not include the species in its list of County reptiles encountered during the researchers' field work in the area in the summer of 1930.

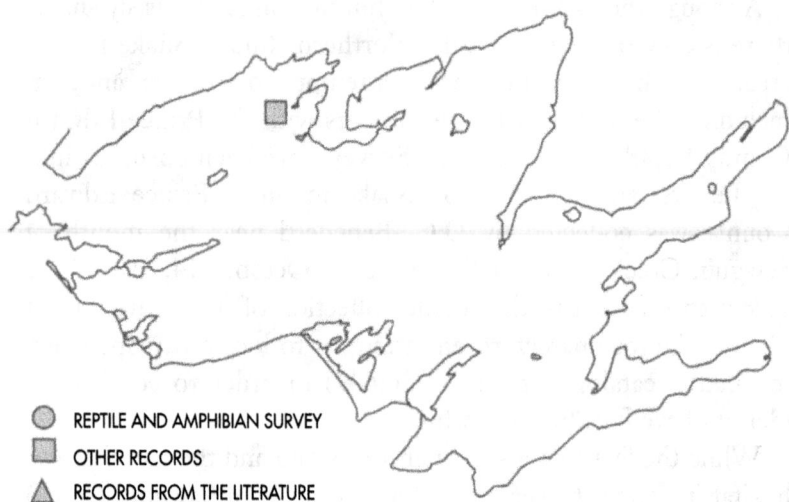

○ REPTILE AND AMPHIBIAN SURVEY
◻ OTHER RECORDS
△ RECORDS FROM THE LITERATURE

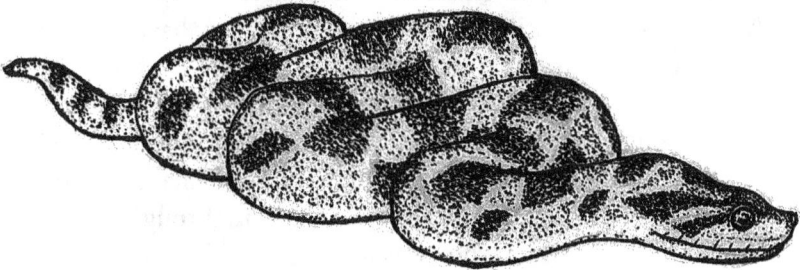

Eastern Hognose Snake
Heterodon platirhinos

Description

This thick-bodied, medium-sized (up to 115.6 cm) snake is best known as a performer of bizarre reptilian theatre.

The Eastern Hognose Snake is most easily recognized by its conspicuous upturned snout. It is also distinguished by its heavy-looking, red-brown-to-grey body with large brown blotches on the back alternating with smaller blotches along the sides. The snake may also appear almost uniformly black.

The Hognose Snake is also recognized by its eccentric behaviour. In fact, its peculiar response to danger has earned it such ominous-sounding monikers as the "puff adder" or the "blow viper." When confronted, the snake flattens its head, hissing loudly, and fills its body fat with air. If this impressive demonstration fails, it rolls suddenly onto its back, feigning death. The Eastern Hognose Snake prefers sandy areas, where it may be found prowling slowly for frogs and toads.

Distribution

The Eastern Hognose Snake is most certainly a hypothetical species for Prince Edward County; that is, encountering one in the area would be a rare occurrence.

While this species' range appears to reach east to include the County, only one record of the Eastern Hognose Snake exists for the area. Past and recent investigations of Prince Edward County wildlife, including the work of researchers with the Prince Edward County Reptile and Amphibian Survey, have failed to uncover any other sighting of the species.

The first and only Eastern Hognose Snake record for Prince Edward County was reported at the Sandbanks on June 6, 1969 by amateur herpetologist Lubomyr Luciuk. The snake, estimated to be about 45 cm long, was described going through its characteristic feigning ritual when it was confronted by the observer.

There are reasons to be sceptical of the record. Principal among these is the absence of any other report of this slow, conspicuous and easily identified snake, particularly from the well-trod vicinity of Sandbanks Park. Also, Michael Oldham of the Ontario Herpetofaunal Summary points out that "the species is not known from other suitable sites nearby," like Presqu'ile Park northwest of the County.

On the other hand, Francis R. Cook, former head of herpetology at the Canadian Museum of Nature, reports that he knew the observer responsible for the record to be quite familiar with indigenous reptiles and amphibians. Further, the Eastern Hognose Snake would be very difficult to confuse with another species for such an experienced observer. Cook also points out that evidence of the presence of Hognose Snakes in the County may shed some light on earlier reports of Eastern Massasauga (*Sistrurus catenatus catenatus*) in the area; the former's behaviour could easily lead some to believe it was a rattlesnake.

There is no mention of the Eastern Hognose Snake in the Ontario Ministry of Natural Resources' 1973 *Ecological and Geological Overview of Prince Edward County*. Similarly, the Royal Ontario Museum's 1941 *Faunal Investigation of Prince Edward County, Ontario* makes does not include the species in its list of County reptiles.

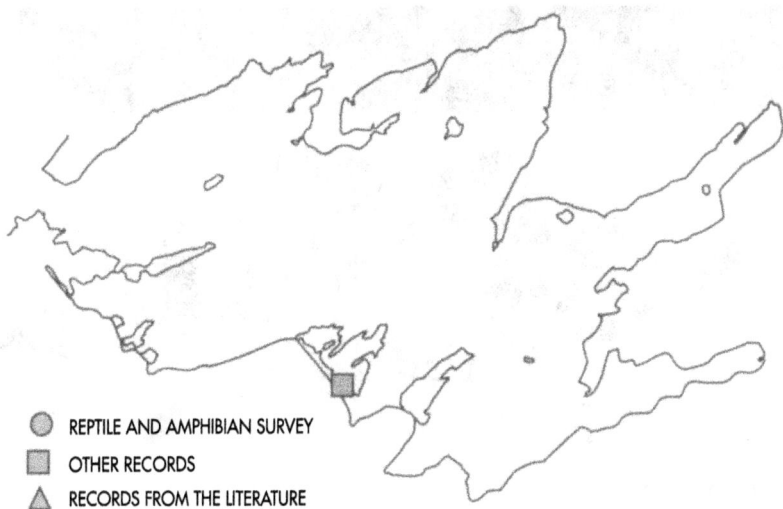

◯ REPTILE AND AMPHIBIAN SURVEY
▢ OTHER RECORDS
△ RECORDS FROM THE LITERATURE

Black Rat Snake
Elaphe obsoleta obsoleta

Description

This impressive and largest of Ontario snakes (up to 256.5 cm) may be included here only as a consequence of a case of mistaken identity.

The Black Rat Snake's plain, shiny black appearance is its most distinguishing characteristic. The chin and throat of the snake is creamy white and the belly is dusky grey with some checkerboard-like markings. Occasionally, traces of large darker spots are visible on the back. The Black Rat Snake prefers old pastures, farmyard clearings or along the edges of open woodlands. The snakes appetite for eggs and nestlings as well as its skill at climbing make finding one in a tree a strong possibility.

Distribution

The Black Rat Snake is included here as a hypothetical species for Prince Edward County and almost certainly does not currently occur in the area today, if it ever did.

The only records of this species in Prince Edward County are anecdotal and considerably dated. Other more recent investigations of Prince Edward County wildlife, including the work of researchers with the Prince Edward County Reptile and Amphibian Survey, have failed to uncover any other sighting of the species in the area.

The reports that do exist for the Black Rat Snake in the County are described in the Royal Ontario Museum's 1941 *Faunal Investigation of Prince Edward County, Ontario*. The reports note the observations of area resident W.J. Palmer who described the Black Rat Snake as "common at North Port." The same observer told the researchers he found the snake once at an old well in a field near Picton. The investigation points to the well-documented occurrence of the Black Rat Snake in nearby Frontenac County as lending "weight" to the Prince Edward County records. Unfortunately, the possibility of inexperienced observers misidentifying large, near-black Northern Water Snakes (*Nerodia sipedon sipedon*) as Black Rat Snakes detracts from the sightings. Northern Water Snakes are common in Prince Edward County.

The so-called proximity to Prince Edward County of the only population of Black Rat Snakes currently known in eastern Ontario does little to support the possibility of the snakes living or having lived in the area. The colony of Black Rat Snakes thriving along the edge of the Canadian Shield in the Frontenac County is notable for its isolation and clearly defined boundaries. Francis Cook, former head of herpetology at the Canadian Museum of Nature, notes that the snakes, while quite common within their localized range in Frontenac County, are absent just outside that range.

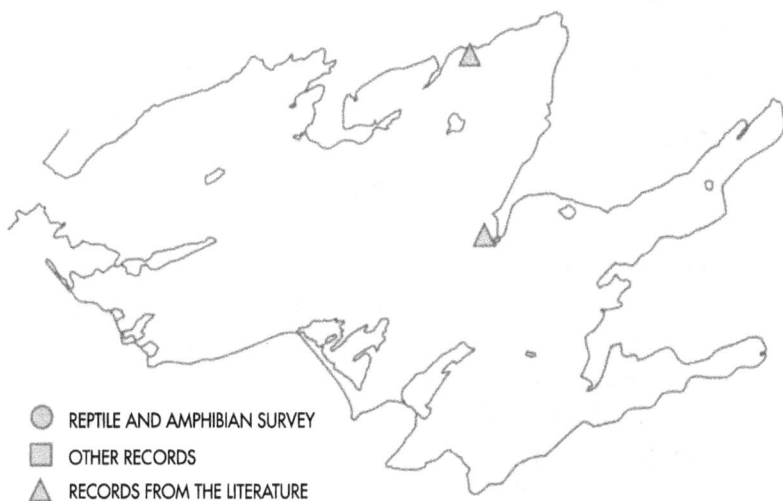

○ REPTILE AND AMPHIBIAN SURVEY
▢ OTHER RECORDS
△ RECORDS FROM THE LITERATURE

Eastern Massasauga
Sistrurus catenatus catenatus

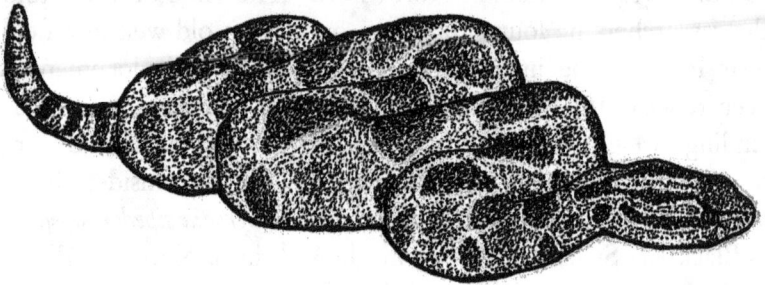

Description

This medium-sized (up to 100.3 cm), venomous snake is more a denizen of Prince Edward County lore than a resident of the County itself.

The Eastern Massasauga is a grey to brown rattlesnake with black or dark-brown blotches down the back and rows of smaller patches down the side. A brown rattle is usually easily spotted at the end of the snake's tail. Another distinguishing characteristic is the snake's vertical, narrow pupils. If encountered at all, the Eastern Massasauga would likely be found in clearings or along the edges of woodlands close to open water or swampy areas.

Distribution

The Eastern Massasauga is almost certainly extirpated in Prince Edward County, if it ever occurred in the area. The rattlesnake is currently considered "threatened" both nationally and provincially by the Committee on the Status of Endangered Wildlife in Canada (COSEWIC) and by the Ontario Ministry of Natural Resources respectively.

All records of this species in Prince Edward County are very old—from the late 1700s through to 1929—and all are infuriatingly more anecdotal than carefully documented. Where specific locations are mentioned, the reports suggest the rattlesnake was historically found near Demorestville, Consecon, North Port and West Lake. More recent faunal investigations of these areas and of the rest of Prince Edward County, including the work of researchers with the Prince Edward County Reptile and Amphibian Survey, have failed to uncover more recent reports of the species.

The Royal Ontario Museum's 1941 *Faunal Investigation of Prince Edward County, Ontario* includes the most comprehensive list of records for the Massasauga in the area. The most recent of these is a report from area resident W.J. Palmer that he killed two near Demorestville in 1929. The investigation also mentions a story told by W.H. Lunn, another resident, of a pioneer named Lieutenant Paul Trumpour who felt forced to give up his farm near Consecon in the late 1700s because of the abundance of rattlesnakes. A 1937 letter from the same resident to the Royal Ontario Museum researchers describes a rattlesnake killed at North Port at about 1912 by Don Fraser and another killed there in 1928 or 1929 by Albert Rowe.

Another letter written to the investigators by Grant Carman in 1937 describes the rattlesnake as "nearly extinct but they were certainly numerous years ago." The same letter says an isolated population on a small island in West Lake was nevertheless doing well. The writer mentions that his father killed one (68 cm) in 1925 or 1926. An even earlier record mentions the presence of the Eastern Massasauga in the County on July 7, 1814.

There is other circumstantial evidence suggesting the rattlesnake was resident, if not abundant in Prince Edward County. First, the Ontario Herpetofaunal Summary has compiled a number of historic records for the species for a variety of other areas across the south of the province. Further, some geological features in the northern portions of the County bear names that suggest rattlesnakes may have been part of the area's heritage, such as Massasauga Point on Huff's Island and Rattlesnake Creek near Carrying Place.

As Michael Oldham of the Ontario Herpetofaunal Summary points out, "The species seems to have been eliminated in much of southern Ontario over a century ago." If it ever occurred in the area, Prince Edward County was not likely an exception in this widespread extermination of the province's only venomous snake.

It is worth mentioning, however, that a number of snake species are known to occasionally "rattle" their tail when threatened, often producing a rattling sound if their vibrating tails brush dried leaves or other appropriate material. Eastern Milk Snakes (*Lampropeltis triangulum triangulum*), Northern Water Snakes (*Nerodia sipedon sipedon*) and even Eastern Garter Snakes (*Thamnophis sirtalis sirtalis*) have all been known to attempt this apparent mimicry and all occur in the County. These may have been responsible for some of the earlier accounts of Eastern Massasaugas in the area. A lone report of an Eastern Hognose Snake at the Sandbanks in 1969 also raises the possibility that this species—well known for its dramatic, threatening behaviour—may have been earlier mistaken for a rattlesnake.

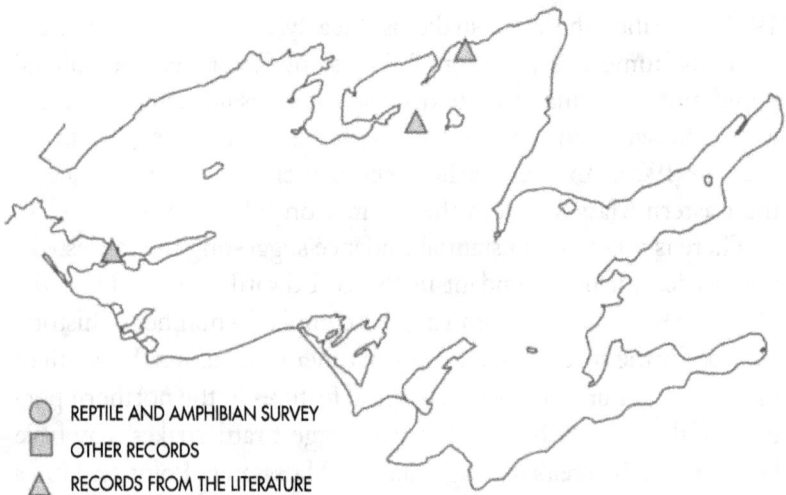

○ REPTILE AND AMPHIBIAN SURVEY
▢ OTHER RECORDS
△ RECORDS FROM THE LITERATURE

Pickerel Frog
Rana palustris

Description

This medium-sized (up to 8.7 cm), spotted frog is one of Prince Edward County's most elusive amphibians.

The Pickerel Frog is recognized by the two rows of dark, irregular, squarish spots running down the length of its brown or green back. It also has similar marks on its sides and two light-coloured ridges running along either side of the back. The similarity of appearance between this species and the Northern Leopard Frog (*Rana pipiens*) make identification difficult. In some cases, the Pickerel Frog can be distinguished by its squared marks. Its call is a low snore and can be heard from March through to June. If encountered at all, the Pickerel Frog is most likely found in cool, usually clear pools, ponds and streams.

Distribution

The Pickerel Frog is a hypothetical species for Prince Edward County, meaning that it is very uncommon, if not absent from the area.

While the County appears to be within the range for this frog, there are few records and a couple of other inconclusive references to the species in the area. Other attempts to track down a Pickerel Frog on the island, including those of the Prince Edward County Reptile and Amphibian Survey, have been unsuccessful.

The Reptile and Amphibian Survey's report noted what it considered a reliable account by an unnamed area naturalist of a lone Pickerel Frog calling on May 29, 1979 at Big Island Marsh and another account of several being found at East Lake in August of that year.

Prince Edward County's only Pickerel Frog specimen was collected by D.C. Benedetti near where Highway 62 crosses Sawguin Creek on October 14, 1979. The specimen was sent to the reptile collection of the University of Guelph. Unfortunately, recent attempts to locate this specimen (collection catalogue number UG 648) in order to confirm its identity have been unsuccessful.

While the fact that a specimen was taken in this last instance and the fact that the habitat in which the frog was found (that is, at Sawguin Creek) both add to the veracity of the record, there may be reasons to doubt it. The most obvious of these is the frog's resemblance to the Northern Leopard Frog (*Rana pipiens*) which can make distinguishing between the two very difficult for most observers. The second reason for scepticism is the unlikely coincidence that the same collector captured the County's only known specimen of the Northern Ribbon Snake (*Thamnophis sauritus septentrionalis*)—also sent to the University of Guelph and also unaccounted for.

However, there are other records. In his wetland evaluation of the Big Island Marsh, Jon Boxall, working as a biological consultant for the Ontario Ministry of Natural Resources, reported finding a Pickerel Frog at that location on August 24, 1993. Field notes accompanying the evaluation offer no clue as to how the frog was distinguished. Thomas A. Huff of the Reptile Breeding Foundation recalled that in 1993 he collected two frogs from the same area whose appearance closely matched the description for Pickerel Frog. Further attempts to definitively identify the frogs at his home were, however, inconclusive. There is no mention of the Pickerel Frog in the Ontario Ministry of Natural Resources' 1973 *Ecological and Geological Overview of Prince Edward County*.

Older records suggesting the Pickerel Frog was once resident in Prince Edward County also exist in the literature. While researchers with the Royal Ontario Museum's 1941 *Faunal Investigation of Prince Edward County, Ontario* also found no evidence of the Pickerel Frog during their work in the area in 1930, they note that area naturalist W.J. LeRay reported finding the species at Cressy in 1938 and 1939, but that it was "not common there."

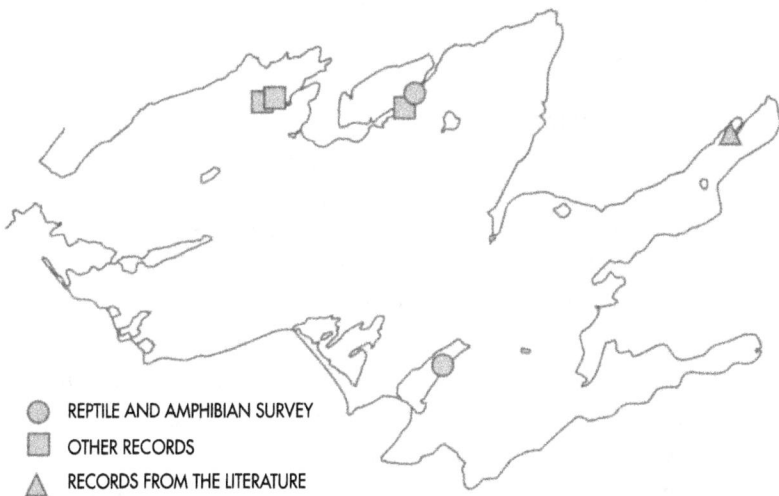

⬤ REPTILE AND AMPHIBIAN SURVEY
◻ OTHER RECORDS
△ RECORDS FROM THE LITERATURE

OTHER HYPOTHETICAL SPECIES

The reptiles and amphibians selected for discussion in this book are those for which there are (generally) first-hand records of their occurrence in Prince Edward County. These may be contemporary or historic. In the course of compiling this information, however, I repeatedly uncovered accounts of other reptile and amphibian species that were related as second- or third-hand reports of (usually) uncertain observations. Among these, stories of the suspected or possible presence of Eastern Spiny Softshell Turtles (*Apalone spinifera spinifera*), Wood Turtles (*Clemmys insculpta*), Four-Toed Salamanders (*Hemidactylium scutatum*) and Mink Frogs (*Rana septentrionalis*) deserve mention here. I will deal with the most compelling accounts first.

Michael Oldham of the Ontario Herpetofaunal Summary has uncovered records for the Four-Toed Salamander as close as Presqu'ile Provincial Park near Prince Edward County's northwest corner. This small, woodland species, distinguished by its reddish back, white speckled belly and sides and four-toed hind feet, has never been found within the borders of Prince Edward County despite the intensive investigations over the years. But the proximity of the Presqu'ile records suggest that this small, inconspicuous animal may turn up during future searches of suitable boggy woodlands (particularly where sphagnum moss is found) within the County, especially in the northwest corner.

Similarly intriguing perhaps are three reports of Wood Turtles found near Salmon Point by different observers on separate occasions in the early 1980s. All were related by Thomas Huff, formerly of the Reptile Breeding Foundation, who recalled that two of the people who encountered the turtles were familiar with the species, if not with the significance of finding the animals in this area. However, Wood Turtles, a mainly terrestrial brown turtle with a rough, high-domed, tortoise-like shell, are popular pets and the proximity of this site to the Sandbanks Provincial Park (a frequently visited tourist site) points to the likelihood that these animals were escapees or had been released by tourists. Francis Cook, formerly of the Canadian Museum of Nature, also notes that young Blanding's Turtles (*Emydoidea blandingii*) have been mistaken for Wood Turtles by even experienced observers. Prince Edward County is far outside the Wood Turtle's range as we currently understand it, so it is unlikely that these were indigenous in the County. The Wood Turtle is currently considered "vulnerable" both nationally and provincially by the Committee on the Status of Endangered Wildlife in Canada (COSEWIC) and by the Ontario Ministry of Natural Resources respectively.

Of other stories of other species, some were discounted after a little investigation. For instance, reports that a conservation officer in Belleville had seen Eastern Spiny Softshell Turtles being pulled from the nets of fishermen on the Trent Canal near Carrying Place was dispelled with a simple call to the officer in question. The Spiny Softshell Turtle is currently considered "threatened" both nationally and provincially by the Committee on the Status of Endangered Wildlife in Canada (COSEWIC) and by the Ontario Ministry of Natural Resources respectively.

Similarly, two Prince Edward County records for the Mink Frog included by consultants in the Ontario Ministry of Natural Resources wetland surveys at Black River and Wellers Bay proved to be mistaken after the two observers to whom the reports were attributed could not recall making them. The range for the Mink Frog in Ontario is typically more northerly, following the edge of the Canadian Shield. The frog's superficial resemblance to the Green Frog (*Rana clamitans melanota*) makes cases of mistaken identity common.

AFTERWORD

The human imagination's vilification of reptiles and amphibians is a tradition that stretches back almost as long as the existence of the animals themselves. For instance, the snake wears the black hat in the Book of Genesis, and the frog is a pestilence in Exodus. The lowly toad, meanwhile, is the odious centrepiece in many a traditional fairy tale. Over a very long time, the reputation of these mainly harmless animals has endured more slings and arrows than St. Sebastian. As a self-appointed publicist for these creatures—animals that may have had more to do with the germination of my interest in natural history than any others—I find this fact a little troubling; they are fascinating and, in many cases, beautiful beasts and deserve their infamy less than many people I know.

But the historic tendency to view reptiles and amphibians unfavourably is less concerning by far than the modern one to ignore their ecologically sensitive world altogether.

The short history of Prince Edward County since the time of its settlement has its own chapters devoted to the punishment of the area's environment by the march of development. One obvious historic example is suggested by the old records that indicate the Eastern Massasauga (*Sistrurus catenatus catenatus*) may have existed in the north of the County before being extirpated completely from the area by settlers.

But the lessons of the distant past are nothing compared to the lessons we are learning now or have yet to learn about changes in populations of County reptiles and amphibians and their frightening portent of dramatic environmental and wetland degradation. For instance, the 1979 Reptile and Amphibian Survey of Prince Edward County found what it described as "a small percentage" of the Northern Leopard Frog (*Rana pipiens*) population had foot deformities (ie. extra toes, forked toes or toes joined together), a clear illustration widespread groundwater pollution in the area. Equally chilling was the smaller number of Green Frogs (*Rana clamitans melanota*) found by the survey team without irises or with other eye anomalies.

These phenomena should make us pause. Attention needs to be paid to the changes taking place in our reptile and amphibian populations as residential and industrial development continues apace. The unique life cycles and sensitivities of these animals—existing as they do with their ears to the ground, so to speak—make them valuable environmental voices. They need to be heard.

The Ontario Herpetofaunal Summary provides a good example of a systematic attempt to listen. By continuing to collect any and all records of Ontario reptiles and amphibians, the summary is beginning to paint an important picture of the shifts taking place within the province's reptile and amphibian communities. Similarly, the Long Point Bird Observatory's Marsh Monitoring Program is another good example of an attempt to measure changes in the voices of wetlands throughout Ontario. Volunteers with this program repeatedly visit wetland sites to note any changes in the vigour of singing birds and frogs.

These and others represent the kinds of effort that need to be devoted to these animals if we want to understand what subtle and accumulated effects the changes to our environment are having and what they may mean in the long run. The fact is that while maligning these slithery and slippery animals may be something of a tradition, they may have something important to say to us about the state of our land and water; these so-called villains may yet become heroes in their role as coal mine canaries.

REFERENCES

Anthony, L. 1991. The Kingdom of Spring. *Seasons* 31(1): 26-32.

Briggs, P. 1979. *A Preliminary Report on the 1979 Survey of Reptiles and Amphibians of Prince Edward County.* Unpublished. 16 pp.

Cadman, M.D., P.F.J. Eagles and F.M. Helleiner. 1987. *Atlas of Breeding Birds of Ontario.* University of Waterloo Press, Waterloo. 617 pp.

Conant, R and J.T. Collins. 1991. *A Field Guide to Reptiles and Amphibians, Eastern and Central North America.* 3rd Ed. Houghton Mifflin Co., New York. 450 pp.

Cook, F.R. 1984. *Introduction to Canadian Amphibians and Reptiles.* National Museums of Canada, Ottawa. 200 pp.

Crowder, A.A., B. McLaughlin, R.D. Weir, W.J. Christie. 1986. Shoreline Fauna of the Bay of Quinte. p. 190-200. In C.K. Minns, D.A. Hurley and K.H. Nicholls [eds.] *Project Quinte: Point-Source Phosphorous Control and Ecosystem Response in the Bay of Quinte, Lake Ontario.* Can. Spec. Publ. Fish. Aquat. Sci. 86: 270 pp.

Glooschenko, V., B. Parker, L. Coo, R. Kent, C. Wedeles, A. Mason, J. Dawson, D. Herman, P. Smith. 1988. *Provincially and Regionally Significant Wetlands in Southern Ontario, Interim Report-1987.* Wildlife Branch, Ontario Ministry of Natural Resources, Queen's Park, Toronto. 321 pp.

Johnson, B. 1989. *Familiar Amphibians and Reptiles of Ontario.* Natural Heritage/Natural History Inc., Toronto. 168 pp.

MacDonald, I.D. 1987. *Life Science Areas of Natural and Scientific Interest in Site District 6-5.* Parks and Recreation Areas Sector, Ontario Ministry of Natural Resources, Eastern Region, Kemptville. 149 pp.

Norris, T. and D. Cuddy. 1990. *An Evaluation of Life Science Resources of Sandbanks Provincial Park.* Ontario Ministry of Natural Resources, Eastern Region, Kingston.

Oldham, J.C. and H.M. Smith. 1991. The Genetic Status of the Smooth Green Snake, *Opheodrys vernalis. Bulletin of the Maryland Herpetological Society* 27(4): 201-215.

Prince Edward Region Conservation Authority. 1968. *Prince Edward Region Conservation Report.* Conservation Authorities Branch, Department of Energy and Resources Management, Toronto. 161 pp.

Snyder, L.L., E.B.S. Logier, T.B. Kurata, F.A. Urquhart and J.F Brimley. 1941. *A Faunal Investigation of Prince Edward County, Ontario.* University of Toronto Press, Toronto. 123 pp.

Whitcombe, M., R. Harris and R.J. Carlisle. 1973. *An Ecological and Geological Overview of Prince Edward County 1973.* Park Planning Branch, Environmental Planning Section, Ontario Ministry of Natural Resources, Queen's Park, Toronto. 415 pp.

APPENDIX A
A Checklist of County Reptiles and Amphibians

Common Snapping Turtle *Chelydra serpentina serpentina*
Common Musk Turtle *Sternotherus odoratus*
Common Map Turtle *Graptemys geographica*
Midland Painted Turtle *Chrysemys picta marginata*
Blanding's Turtle *Emydoidea blandingii*

Northern Water Snake *Nerodia sipedon sipedon*
Brown Snake *Storeria dekayi*
Northern Redbelly Snake *Storeria occipitomaculata occipitomaculata*
Eastern Garter Snake *Thamnophis sirtalis sirtalis*
Northern Ribbon Snake *Thamnophis sauritus septentrionalis*
Eastern Hognose Snake *Heterodon platirhinos*
Northern Ringneck Snake *Diadophis punctatus edwardsii*
Smooth Green Snake *Opheodrys vernalis (Liochlorophis vernalis)*
Black Rat Snake *Elaphe obsoleta obsoleta*
Eastern Milk Snake *Lampropeltis triangulum triangulum*
Eastern Massasauga *Sistrurus catenatus catenatus*

Mudpuppy *Necturus maculosus maculosus*
Spotted Salamander *Ambystoma maculatum*
Blue-Spotted/Jefferson Salamander *Ambystoma*
    laterale-jeffersonianum complex
Red-Spotted Newt *Notophthalmus viridescens viridescens*
Redback Salamander *Plethodon cinereus*

Eastern American Toad *Bufo americanus americanus*
Grey Treefrog *Hyla versicolor*
Northern Spring Peeper *Pseudacris crucifer crucifer*
Western Chorus Frog *Pseudacris triseriata triseriata*
Bullfrog *Rana catesbeiana*
Green Frog *Rana clamitans melanota*
Wood Frog *Rana sylvatica*
Northern Leopard Frog *Rana pipiens*
Pickerel Frog *Rana palustris*

APPENDIX B
Singing Periods of County Frogs

Note: Grey Treefrogs (*Hyla versicolor*), Western Chorus Frogs (*Pseudacris triseriata triseriata*), Northern Spring Peepers (*Pseudacris crucifer crucifer*) and Wood Frogs (*Rana sylvatica*) all occasionally call in the autumn, often on warm, wet days, well after their breeding season has finished. These calls are often solitary and usually far from the breeding site. They are distinguished here as "fall calls" and separated from breeding calls.

	April	May	June	July	August
Eastern American Toad	12 April 1988 (earliest call)	29 May 1995 (first full chorus)	30 June 1930 (latest breeding call)		
Grey Treefrog	19 April 1976 (earliest call)	15 June 1979 (first full chorus)	28 June 1988 (latest breeding call)		17 October 1987 (latest "fall call")
Spring Peeper	1 April 1988 (earliest call) / 30 April 1988 (first full chorus)		11 June 1930 (latest breeding call)		5 September 1987 (latest "fall call")
Western Chorus Frog	15 March 1990 (earliest call) / 9 April 1993 (first full chorus)	30 May 1994 (latest breeding call)			29 October 1989 (latest "fall call")
Bullfrog		12 May 1979 (earliest call)			10 August 1979 (latest call)
Green Frog		5 May 1993 (earliest call)			2 August 1979 (latest call)
Wood Frog	30 March 1995 (earliest call)	15 May 1985 (latest call)			
Northern Leopard Frog	21 March 1987 (earliest call) / 15 April 1976 (earliest first full chorus)			25 July 1979 (latest call)	
Pickerel Frog		29 May 1979 (one call record)			

APPENDIX C
A List of Museum Specimens

The following list of specimens is primarily drawn from the database of the Ontario Herpetofaunal Summary and the data of the Prince Edward County Reptile and Amphibian Survey. The museum acronyms are as follows: NMC—National Museum of Canada (now the Canadian Museum of Nature), Ottawa, Ont.; ROM—Royal Ontario Museum, Toronto, Ont.; UG—University of Guelph, Guelph, Ont.; UMMZ—University of Michigan Museum of Zoology, Ann Arbor, Mi.; WLU—Wilfred Laurier University, Waterloo, Ont.; NBM—University of New Brunswick, St. John, N.B.

Species	Museum	Cat.#	Collection	Location	Date
Common Snapping Turtle	NMC	20555		Garrett Island	22 Aug. 1979
	NMC	19527	1 adult	West Lake	18 May 1979
	NMC	19343		Black River	8 Aug. 1979
Common Map Turtle	NMC	19350		Outlet	7 June 1978
	NMC	27225		East Lake	? 1978
Midland Painted Turtle	NMC	20460		Waring's Creek	27 June 1979
	NMC	15003		Consecon Creek	22 Aug. 1972
	ROM	2550, 4154-55, 4162-64	Turtles and eggs	Near Wellington	5 June 1930
	NMC	15007, 15009		Sawguin Creek Marsh	22 Aug. 1972
	NMC	19342	05	Black River	8 Aug. 1979
	NMC	19349		Near Black River	30 May 1978

Species	Museum	Cat.#	Collection	Location	Date
Blanding's Turtle	ROM	7358		Wellington	? Aug. 1943
	NMC	19351		Cherry Valley	22 July 1978
	NMC	19352		Long Point	3 Aug. 1978
	ROM	2596		Waupoos Island	14 July 1928
Northern Water Snake	NMC	18932		Massasauga Point	? May 1973
	NMC	20557		Near Keller's Creek	20 Aug. 1979
	NMC	14333		Milford	1 May 1971
	NMC	26295		Black River	4 Oct. 1980
	ROM	4152		Cressy	2 July 1930
	ROM	1826		Main Duck Island	5 July 1928
Brown Snake	ROM	2433		Garrett Island	5 July 1930
	NMC	20463		Near East Lake	25 June 1979
	ROM	2380		Near East Lake	11 July 1930
	NMC	26292		Near North Port	6 Oct. 1977
	NMC	25017		Near Milford (?)	27 Sept. 1983
Northern Redbelly Snake	NMC	20529		Near Keller's Creek	17 Sept. 1979
Eastern Garter Snake	NMC	?	2 adults	West Lake	7 July 1985
	ROM	2474		West Lake	3 June 1930
	NMC	15004		Consecon Creek	22 Aug. 1972

Species	Museum	Cat.#	Collection	Location	Date
	ROM	2465-71, 2475-77		Near Wellington	27 May 1930
	NMC	28473		Near Cherry Valley	31 May 1986
	NMC	26293		Near Milford	25 Aug. 1980
	ROM	2472		Near Cressy	2 July 1930
	NMC	20554		McMahon Bluff	21 Aug. 1979
	NMC	14332		Milford	1 May 1979
	NMC	12760		Glenora	11 May 1968
	ROM	2437		Lake-On -The-Mountain	29 June 1930
	NMC	19341		Little Bluff	14 Aug. 1979
	ROM	1825		Main Duck Island	5 July 1928
	NMC	20580		Main Duck Island	14 July 1979
Northern Ribbon Snake (unconfirmed)	UG	647		Sawguin Creek Marsh	14 Oct. 1979
Northern Ringneck Snake	NMC	25006		Outlet	3 June 1983
	NMC	24988		Lost Lake	2 Aug. 1982
Eastern Milk Snake	ROM	2689		Consecon Lake	? 1930
	UG	650		Sawguin Creek Marsh	11 Sept. 1979
	NMC	20401		Near East Lake	1 June 1979

Species	Museum	Cat.#	Collection	Location	Date
	NMC	20404		Near Milford	11 May 1979
	NMC	25019		Near Milford	29 Sept. 1983
	NMC	1175		Picton	4 July 1925
	ROM	6855		Picton	14 May 1942
	NMC	20490		Little Bluff	28 June 1979
	NMC	20402		Glenora	19 May 1979
	NMC	?		Keller's Creek	21 Aug. 1979
Mudpuppy	ROM	2656		Near Wellington	? May 1930
Blue-Spotted/ Jefferson Salamander	ROM	2455		Garrett Island	23 May 1930
	ROM	2456		West Lake	23 May 1930
	ROM	2655		Near Wellington	? May 1932
	NMC	19522	8	Outlet	18 June 1979
	NMC	20560	4	Near Black River	30 Aug. 1979
	NMC	20549		Glenora	24 Aug. 1979
	NMC	22671		Woodville	23 Aug. 1979
	NMC	22672-73		Lost Lake	24 Aug. 1979
Hybrid	ROM	H11300		Near Milford	10 Oct. 1979
Hybrid Confirmed	ROM	10670-71	7 "Tremblay's"	Cherry Valley	28 Sept. 1978
	ROM	10693-94	6 "Tremblay's"	Cherry Valley	11 Nov. 1978
Spotted Salamander	ROM	2546	4 larvae	Picton	28 June 1930
	NMC	19412		Near Black River	30 Aug. 1979

Species	Museum	Cat.#	Collection	Location	Date
Red-Spotted Newt	ROM	2551	8 specimens	Near Wellington	23 May 1930
	ROM	2427		Near Picton	28 June 1930
	NMC	20543 -44	8 adults	Lake-On-The-Mountain	16 Aug. 1979
	NMC	20550	5 adults	Lake-On-The-Mountain	24 Aug. 1979
	NMC	20355	6	Black River	10 July 1979
	NMC	20411	1 larva	Keller's Creek	18 July 1979
	NMC	14278		Smith Bay	31 July 1972
	NMC	20493	9 larvae	Near Green Point	29 June 1979
	NMC	20506	3 larvae	Long Point	26 July 1979
	NMC	20499	5 larvae	Long Point	4 July 1979
	NMC	20505	6	Long Point	18 July 1979
	NMC	20501	2 larvae	Long Point	11 July 1979
	NMC	20532	13	Timber Island	24 July 1979
Redback Salamander	ROM	2452-54 2463, 3664		Garrett Island	3 July 1930
	ROM	2436-51		Garrett Island	23 May 1930
	ROM	2457-60		Near Wellington	2 June 1930
	ROM	2462		Near Wellington	20 June 1930
	NMC	14283		Milford	31 July 1972
	NMC	20558		Waring Creek	28 Aug. 1979
	NMC	20551	25	Glenora	24 Aug. 1979
	NMC	20545	2	Glenora	16 Aug. 1979
	NMC	20556		Lake-On-The-Mountain	23 Aug. 1979

Species	Museum	Cat.#	Collection	Location	Date
American Toad	NMC	20374	24 tadpoles	Hubb's Creek	1 June 1979
	NMC	20379	40 tadpoles	Consecon Creek	1 June 1979
	NMC	19485	10 tadpoles	Sandbanks	17 May 1979
	NMC	19489	1 adult, 36 tadpoles	Sandbanks	20 June 1979
	NMC	20459	7	West Lake	25 June 1979
	ROM	2422-23		Sandbanks	5 July 1930
	NMC	19486	14 tadpoles	Sandbanks	12 June 1979
	NMC	19496	1	Sandbanks	28 June 1979
	NMC	20445		Near Allisonville	11 May 1979
	NMC	20473	2 tadpoles	Near Wellington	18 July 1979
	NMC	20479	2 tadpoles	Near Wellington	25 July 1979
	NMC	19543	41 tadpoles	Yerexville	22 May 1979
	NMC	19537	18 tadpoles	Yerexville	13 June 1979
	NMC	19540	7 tadpoles	Yerexville	29 June 1979
	ROM	2424		Near Picton	27 June 1930
	NMC	20347	17 tadpoles	Near Big Swamp	24 May 1979
	NMC	20344	20 tadpoles	Near Woodville	24 May 1979
	NMC	20346	11 tadpoles	Near Woodville	12 June 1979
	NMC	20342	4 tadpoles	Green Point	23 May 1979
	NMC	19546	4 tadpoles	Yerexville	13 June 1979
	NMC	19550	1	Yerexville	21 June 1979
	NMC	20304	2 froglets	Yerexville	29 June 1979
	NMC	20309	1	Yerexville	5 July 1979
	NMC	20392	45 tadpoles	Near Petticoat Point	6 June 1979

Species	Museum	Cat.#	Collection	Location	Date
	NMC	20393	58 tadpoles	Near Petticoat Point	15 June 1979
	NMC	20394	21 tadpoles	Near Petticoat Point	20 June 1979
	NMC	20395	5 froglets	Near Petticoat Point	28 June 1979
	NMC	20396	5 tadpoles	Near Petticoat Point	11 July 1979
	NMC	14280		Black River	31 July 1972
	NMC	20403	33 tadpoles	Keller's Creek	17 June 1979
	NMC	20412	1 adult	Keller's Creek	28 July 1979
	NMC	19483	10 tadpoles	Near Keller's Creek	16 May 1979
	NMC	20382	9 tadpoles	Near Keller's Creek	5 June 1979
	NMC	20383	25 tadpoles	Near Keller's Creek	18 June 1979
	NMC	20329	4 tadpoles	Near Fish Lake	23 May 1979
	NMC	20332	3	Near Fish Lake	21 June 1979
	NMC	20335	1 tadpole	Near Fish Lake	29 June 1979
	NMC	20340	30 tadpoles	Near Fish Lake	23 May 1979
	NMC	19531	4 tadpoles	Near Green Point	21 June 1979
	NMC	20423		Little Bluff	19 June 1979
	NMC	20385	1 tadpole	Cape Vese	6 June 1979
	ROM	1495		Near Waupoos	18 July 1928
	ROM	3199		Prinyer's Cove	3 July 1912
Grey Treefrog	NMC	19491	1 tadpole	Sandbanks	20 June 1979

Species	Museum	Cat.#	Collection	Location	Date
	NMC	19498	35	Sandbanks	28 June 1979
	NMC	19500	1 tadpole	Sandbanks	6 July 1979
	NMC	19502	4 tadpoles	Sandbanks	13 July 1979
	NMC	19505	1 tadpole	Sandbanks	29 July 1979
	NMC	10508	1 tadpole	Sandbanks	3 Aug. 1979
	NMC	20452	5 froglets	Near Bloomfield	2 Aug. 1979
	NMC	20519	2	Soup Harbour	6 July 1979
	NMC	20364	4 tadpoles	Soup Harbour	12 June 1979
	NMC	16246		Near Outlet	6 Aug. 1972
	NMC	20474	3	Yerexville	18 July 1979
	NMC	20480	3	Yerexville	25 July 1979
	NMC	20483	1 froglet	Yerexville	2 Aug. 1979
	NMC	20305	6 tadpoles	Near Woodville	29 June 1979
	NMC	20310	2	Near Woodville	5 July 1979
	NMC	20314	11 tadpoles	Near Woodville	12 July 1979
	NMC	20317	7	Near Woodville	22 July 1979
	NMC	20320	14	Near Woodville	26 July 1979
	NMC	20323	5	Near Woodville	2 Aug. 1979
	NMC	20537	4 tadpoles	South Bay	1 Aug. 1979
	NMC	20405	1 tadpole	Keller's Creek	8 July 1979
	NMC	20511	2 tadpoles	Near Green Point	5 July 1979
	NMC	20498	4 tadpoles	Little Bluff	4 July 1979
	NMC	20500	10 tadpoles	Little Bluff	11 July 1979
	NMC	20504	8 froglets	Little Bluff	18 July 1979
	NMC	20428	2	Prince Edward Point	19 June 1979

Species	Museum	Cat.#	Collection	Location	Date
Western Chorus Frog	NMC	20377	16 tadpoles	Hubb's Creek	12 June 1979
	NMC	20375, 20380	17, 16 tadpoles	Hubb's Creek	1 June 1979
	NMC	20397	21 tadpoles	Woodrous Corners	8 June 1979
	NMC	19506	1 tadpole	Sandbanks	29 July 1979
	ROM	2545, 2563	58 tadpoles, 25 tadpoles	Near Wellington	23 May 1930
	ROM	2556	58 froglets	Near Wellington	18 June 1930
	NMC	20358	2 tadpoles	Salmon Point	29 May 1979
	NMC	19517, 19513	1 tadpole, 15 tadpoles	Outlet	18 May 1979
	NMC	20361	16 tadpoles	Soup Harbour	29 May 1979
	NMC	20365	22 tadpoles	Soup Harbour	12 June 1979
	NMC	19478	4 tadpoles	Milford	16 May 1979
	ROM	11151, 11161 -62		Cherry Valley	1 Nov. 1978
	NMC	19519	10 tadpoles	Outlet	12 June 1979
	NMC	19521	9 tadpoles	Outlet	20 June 1979
	NMC	19523	6 tadpoles	Outlet	28 June 1979
	NMC	19536	10 tadpoles	Yerexville	22 May 1979
	NMC	19538	1 tadpole	Yerexville	13 June 1979
	NMC	20343	3 tadpoles	Near Fish Lake	23 May 1979
	NMC	20367	6	Near Woodville	23 May 1979
	NMC	19547	19 tadpoles	Near Woodville	13 June 1979
	NMC	20306	21 Tadpoles	Near Woodville	29 June 1979

Species	Museum	Cat.#	Collection	Location	Date
	NMC	20311	6	Near Woodville	5 July 1979
	NMC	19551, 19553	1 tadpole, 20 tadpoles	Near Woodville	21 June 1979
	NMC	20387	9	South Bay	6 June 1979
	NMC	20391	7 tadpoles	South Bay	20 June 1979
	NMC	20398	25 tadpoles	South Bay	8 June 1979
	NMC	20399	31 tadpoles	South Bay	15 June 1979
	NMC	20350	6 tadpoles	Near Lake-On-The-Mountain	28 May 1979
	NMC	20351	11 tadpoles	Near Lake-On-The-Mountain	18 June 1979
	NMC	19479	10 tadpoles	Near Black River	16 May 1979
	NMC	19482	15 tadpoles	Near Keller's Creek	16 May 1979
	NMC	20431, 20443	23 tadpoles, 1	Near Woodville	21 June 1979
	NMC	20341	7 tadpoles	Near Green Point	23 May 1979
	NMC	20559	1	Near Gravelly Bay	30 Aug. 1979
	NMC	20420	1	Near Gravelly Bay	18 June 1979
	NMC	20429	2	Prince Edward Point	19 June 1979
Northern Spring Peeper	NMC	19490	16 tadpoles	Sandbanks	20 June 1979
	ROM	2562	36 tadpoles	Garrett Island	10 June 1930
	ROM	2568	4 tadpoles	Sandbanks	25 June 1930

Species	Museum	Cat.#	Collection	Location	Date
	NMC	19495, 19497	17 tadpoles	Sandbanks	28 June 1979
	ROM	2567	1 tadpole	Near Wellington	18 June 1930
	NMC	20518	1	Soup Harbour	6 July 1979
	NMC	19526	2 tadpoles	Outlet	6 July 1979
	ROM	2557	54 tadpoles	Near Picton	28 June 1930
	NMC	20539		South Bay	8 Aug. 1979
	NMC	20333	3 tadpoles	Near Woodville	21 June 1979
	NMC	20336	1 tadpole	Near Woodville	29 June 1979
	NMC	20510	2 tadpoles	Near Green Point	5 June 1979
	NMC	20497	7 tadpoles	Little Bluff	4 July 1979
	ROM	1494		Lost Lake	18 July 1928
Bullfrog	ROM	4147		Near Wellington	24 May 1930
	ROM	2654		Near Wellington	7 July 1932
	NMC	20488	1 tadpole	Beaver Meadow	26 June 1979
	NMC	20388	4	South Bay	6 June 1979
	NMC	20534	1 froglet, 2 tadpoles	Lake-On-The-Mountain	31 July 1979
	NMC	20407	2	Keller's Creek	8 July 1979
	NMC	20409	6 tadpoles	Keller's Creek	15 July 1979
	NMC	20413	16 tadpoles	Keller's Creek	28 July 1979
	NMC	20416	8	Keller's Creek	7 Aug. 1979
	NMC	20418	5 froglets	Keller's Creek	19 Aug. 1979
	NMC	20419	4 tadpoles	Keller's Creek	29 Aug. 1979
	NMC	14279		Smith Bay	31 July 1972
	NMC	20384	1 tadpole	Near Keller's Creek	18 June 1979

Species	Museum	Cat.#	Collection	Location	Date
	NMC	20331	1 tadpole	Near Woodville	12 June 1979
	NMC	20337	1 adult	Near Woodville	29 June 1979
	NMC	20494	2 tadpoles	Near Fish Lake	29 June 1979
	UMMZ	139217	3 tadpoles	Prinyer's Cove	29 May 1928
	ROM	1304		Prinyer's Cove	2 July 1928
Green Frog	ROM	2419		Wellington	4 June 1930
	NMC	20446		Near Allisonville	21 June 1979
	NMC	20447 -48	Several tadpoles	Near Bloomfield	21 June 1979
	NMC	20449	19 tadpoles	Near Bloomfield	12 July 1979
	NMC	20450	14 tadpoles	Near Bloomfield	17 July 1979
	NMC	20451	18 tadpoles	Near Bloomfield	26 July 1979
	NMC	20453	11 tadpoles	Near Bloomfield	2 Aug. 1979
	NMC	20454	19 tadpoles	Near Bloomfield	9 Aug. 1979
	NMC	20455	21 tadpoles	Near Bloomfield	17 Aug. 1979
	NMC	20456	10 tadpoles	Near Bloomfield	23 Aug. 1979
	NMC	15006		Consecon Creek	22 Aug. 1972
	NMC	20520	2 tadpoles	Soup Harbour	6 July 1979
	NMC	19477	1 tadpole	Milford	16 May 1979
	NMC	27552	1 adult	East Lake	6 July 1979
	NMC	20465	3 tadpoles	Yerexville	25 June 1979
	NMC	20471	5 tadpoles	Yerexville	12 July 1979
	NMC	20475-77	2, eggs	Yerexville	18 July 1979
	NMC	20481 -82	1	Yerexville	25 July 1979
	NMC	20484	11 tadpoles	Yerexville	2 Aug. 1979
	NMC	20485		Yerexville	9 Aug. 1979

Species	Museum	Cat.#	Collection	Location	Date
	NMC	19328, 20486		Yerexville	14 Aug. 1979
	NMC	20487		Yerexville	23 Aug. 1979
	NMC	20530	2 tadpoles	Near Picton	19 July 1979
	ROM	2416, 2418		Near Picton	28 June 1930
	NMC	20522	2 tadpoles	Fish Lake	9 July 1979
	NMC	20538	6 tadpoles	South Bay	1 Aug. 1979
	NMC	20540		South Bay	8 Aug. 1979
	ROM	2412		Near Picton	2 July 1979
	NMC	20349	2 tadpoles	Lake-On-The-Mountain	28 May 1979
	NMC	20546-47	2, 2 tadpoles	Glenora	16 Aug. 1979
	NMC	20356	3 tadpoles	Black River	10 July 1979
	NMC	20535	1 froglet	Lake-On-The-Mountain	31 July 1979
	NMC	20414	1	Keller's Creek	28 July 1979
	NMC	20417	3	Keller's Creek	7 Aug. 1979
	NMC	14277		Smith Bay	31 July 1972
	NMC	20434	1 adult	Near Fish Lake	20 July 1979
	NMC	20437	4 tadpoles	Near Fish Lake	2 Aug. 1979
	NMC	20438	6 tadpoles	Near Fish Lake	12 Aug. 1979
	NMC	20439	8 tadpoles	Near Fish Lake	17 Aug. 1979
	NMC	20440	17	Near Fish Lake	24 Aug. 1979
	NMC	20441	4 tadpoles	Near Fish Lake	29 Aug. 1979
	NMC	20512	1 adult	Near Green Point	5 June 1979
	NMC	19544	2 tadpoles	Near Milford	7 June 1979

Species	Museum	Cat.#	Collection	Location	Date
	NMC	19535	1 tadpole	Near Demorestville	22 May 1979
	NMC	20502	5 tadpoles	Little Bluff	11 July 1979
	UMMZ	66699	1	Prince Edward Bay	24 Aug. 1979
	ROM	3225-27,3233		Near Waupoos	18 July 1928
Wood Frog	NMC	20376, 20381	6 tadpoles	Wellington	1 June 1979
	ROM	2434	1 tadpole	Near Pleasant Bay	4 June 1930
	NMC	20369	16 tadpoles	Near Wellington	30 May 1979
	NMC	20371	1 tadpole	Near Wellington	12 June 1979
	NMC	20528	2 adults	Near Allisonville	18 July 1979
	ROM	2420		Near Wellington	21 June 1930
	ROM	2403-2404		Near Wellington	7 July 1930
	NMC	20366	2 tadpoles	Soup Harbour	12 June 1979
	NMC	19524	1	Outlet	28 June 1979
	NMC	20467	6 froglets	Yerexville	25 June 1979
	NMC	19539	2 tadpoles	Yerexville	13 June 1979
	ROM	2400-02		Near Picton	28 June 1930
	NMC	20345		Near Woodville	24 May 1979
	NMC	19542	6 tadpoles	Yerexville	23 May 1979
	NMC	20581		Keller's Creek	16 Aug. 1979
	NMC	20353	2 tadpoles	Black River	28 May 1979
	NMC	19529	17 tadpoles	Near Green Point	12 June 1979

Species	Museum	Cat.#	Collection	Location	Date
	NMC	19532	7 tadpoles	Near Green Point	21 June 1979
	NMC	20496	10 tadpoles	Near Fish Lake	29 June 1979
	NMC	20432	1 froglet	Near Fish Lake	13 July 1979
	NMC	20436	1 froglet	Near Fish Lake	20 July 1979
	NMC	20424		Little Bluff	19 June 1979
	NMC	429660	2	Near Little Bluff	18 June 1979
	NMC	20422	21 tadpoles	Gravelly Bay	18 June 1979
	ROM	1372	2 tadpoles	Prinyer's Cove	13 June 1928
Northern Leopard Frog	NMC	15005		Wellers Bay	22 Aug. 1972
	NMC	20553	1	North Bay	17 Aug. 1979
	NMC	19329		Huycks Bay	13 Aug. 1979
	NMC	20378	4 tadpoles	North Bay	12 June 1979
	ROM	2405		Near Wellington	4 June 1930
	NMC	20541	1 froglet	Pleasant Bay	13 Aug. 1979
	ROM	2499		Pleasant Bay	1 July 1930
	NMC	19484	20 tadpoles	Sandbanks	17 May 1979
	NMC	19493	15 tadpoles	Sandbanks	20 June 1979
	ROM	2547, 2558	tadpoles	West Lake	9 June 1930
	ROM	2538		Sandbanks	25 June 1930
	ROM	2541		Garrett Island	5 July 1930
	NMC	19488	5 tadpoles	Sandbanks	12 June 1979
	NMC	19499	9	Sandbanks	28 June 1979
	NMC	19501	1 tadpole	Sandbanks	6 July 1979

Species	Museum	Cat.#	Collection	Location	Date
	NMC	19503	14 tadpoles	Sandbanks	13 July 1979
	NMC	19504	4 tadpoles	Sandbanks	22 July 1979
	NMC	19507	7 tadpoles	Sandbanks	29 July 1979
	NMC	19509	1 tadpole	Sandbanks	3 Aug. 1979
	NMC	19510	2 froglets	Sandbanks	12 Aug. 1979
	NMC	19511	3 tadpoles	Sandbanks	19 Aug. 1979
	NMC	19512	3 tadpoles	Sandbanks	22 Aug. 1979
	NMC	27554		West Lake	7 July 1985
	ROM	2482-85		Near Wellington	22 May 1930
	ROM	2540		Near Wellington	7 June 1930
	NMC	15001		Consecon Creek	22 Aug. 1972
	NMC	14334		Mountain View	1 May 1971
	NMC	15008		Sawguin Creek Marsh	22 Aug. 1972
	WLU	6662		Mountain View	4 Sept. 1977
	NMC	20527	2 tadpoles	Big Swamp	17 July 1979
	NMC	20521	4 tadpoles	Soup Harbour	6 July 1979
	NMC	20368	1	Point Petre	29 May 1979
	NMC	20462	11 tadpoles	Woodrous Corners	25 June 1979
	NMC	16245		West Point	6 Aug. 1972
	NMC	27551C		East Lake	6 July 1985
	NMC	20489	1 tadpole	Beaver Meadow	26 June 1979
	NMC	20466	4 tadpoles	Yerexville	25 June 1979
	NMC	20472	5 tadpoles	Yerexville	12 July 1979
	NMC	20478	5	Yerexville	18 July 1979
	NBM	00796	1	Picton	22 Aug. 1971

Species	Museum	Cat.#	Collection	Location	Date
	NMC	19548	18 tadpoles	Yerexville	13 June 1979
	NMC	20307	7 tadpoles	Yerexville	29 June 1979
	NMC	20312	3	Yerexville	5 July 1979
	NMC	20315	2 tadpoles	Yerexville	12 July 1979
	NMC	20318	4	Yerexville	22 July 1979
	NMC	20321	7	Yerexville	26 July 1979
	NMC	20324	6	Yerexville	2 Aug. 1979
	NMC	20326	7	Yerexville	12 Aug. 1979
	NMC	20327	3	Yerexville	17 Aug. 1979
	NMC	19552	7 tadpoles	Yerexville	21 June 1979
	NMC	20509	tadpoles	South Bay	4 July 1979
	NMC	08343		Black River	18 Sept. 1964
	NMC	14282		South Bay	31 July 1972
	NMC	14281		Black River	31 July 1972
	NMC	19331		Black River	3 Aug. 1979
	NMC	20526	1 tadpole	Near Black River	11 July 1979
	NMC	20548	1	Glenora	16 Aug. 1979
	NMC	20552	15 tadpoles	Glenora	24 Aug. 1979
	NMC	20458	16 tadpoles	Near Black River	22 June 1979
	NMC	20408	5 tadpoles	Keller's Creek	8 July 1979
	NMC	20410	7 tadpoles	Keller's creek	15 July 1979
	NMC	20415	6 tadpoles	Keller's Creek	28 July 1979
	NMC	14276		Smith Bay	31 July 1972
	NMC	20330	1 adult	Near Woodville	23 may 1979
	NMC	20334	9 tadpoles	Near Woodville	21 June 1979
	NMC	20338	3 tadpoles	Near Woodville	29 June 1979

Species	Museum	Cat.#	Collection	Location	Date
	NMC	20339	1 froglet	Near Woodville	4 July 1979
	NMC	20495	18 tadpoles	Near Woodville	29 June 1979
	NMC	20444	2 tadpoles	Near Woodville	21 June 1979
	NMC	20433	1 froglet	Near Woodville	13 July 1979
	NMC	20435	3 froglets	Near Woodville	20 July 1979
	NMC	20513 -14	4	Near Fish Lake	5 June 1979
	NMC	20515	2 adults	Near Fish Lake	25 July 1979
	NMC	19533	12 tadpoles	Near Woodville	29 June 1979
	NMC	20526	1 tadpole	Near Black River	11 July 1979
	NMC	20430	6 tadpoles	Prince Edward Point	20 June 1979
	NMC	14284		Prince Edward Point	31 July 1972
	NMC	20523		Main Duck Island	12 July 1979
Pickerel Frog (unconfirmed)	UG	648		Sawguin Creek Marsh	14 Oct. 1979

INDEX

ABOUT THE AUTHOR

Peter Christie is a long-time naturalist and native of Prince Edward County. Before turning his attention to writing, he worked as a researcher for various universities and private foundations, conducting natural history surveys of wildlife in Ontario, Manitoba and Saskatchewan. This work included his participation in a 1979 survey of reptiles and amphibians on which much of this book is based. Most recently, Peter returned to Canada from Tokyo, where he worked as a newspaper editor. His illustrations have appeared in a number of magazines and newspapers in Canada and overseas. Peter considers his ecologist father, the late Jack Christie, to have been his most important guide to the natural world.

Photo: Melanie Willis

9 781896 219271